THE SCIENCE OF OPTIMAL NUTRITION

A Science-Based Approach to Optimize your Nutrition, Avoid and Reverse Chronic diseases and Extend Your Life!

By Dr. William Richardson, M.D., M.S.P.H.

THE SCIENCE OF OPTIMAL NUTRITION

By Dr. William Richardson MD MSPH

Illustrations by: T.D. Mattox
@artbymattox

Front Cover Photo by: Akinbola Richardson
NastyLemonade.com

Book Photos by: Author and Family, except those by Simply Zee Imagery and Mr. Glen Gilkey as indicated.

Editor: Frances Jeffries; Associate Editor: Folasuyi Richardson-Franklin

A Science-Based Approach to Optimize Your Nutrition, Avoid and Reverse Chronic disease and Extend Your Life.

This book contains the opinions and ideas of the author. The intention is to provide helpful information on the subjects herein. Please consult with a competent physician and/or other qualified health care professional for any diagnostic or treatment purposes.

Copyright © 2022 by William Richardson
All rights reserved

ISBN   9781735006024   (softcover)
ASIN   B0B49VZ96F   (e-book)

Dedicated to THE MOST-HIGH, to My Family, and all of My Patients

ACKNOWLEDGEMENTS

My father, Dr. Theodore Roosevelt Richardson, M.D.,
my role model since I was 3 years old.
My loving mother, Lois Virginia Richardson.
Appreciation to all of my Teachers and Professors.

CONTENTS

	Page
INTRODUCTION	7
1. THE SCIENCE OF OPTIMAL NUTRITION	9
2. OPTIMAL NUTRITION: Delicious Plant-based Whole Foods	22
3. HEALTHY PRINCIPLES TO LIVE BY	33
4. NUTRIENT SOURCES IN VEGAN CUISINE	39
5. HEALTHY EATING: Plant-Based Whole Foods	58
6. RECIPES	66
About the Author	116
Resources and Information	118
References	119

INTRODUCTION

Optimal nutrition is crucial to grasp and implement in both industrialized and developing nations to help curtail the pandemic of chronic diseases including heart disease, diabetes, obesity, and cancer engulfing the world today. I am a U.S.-based physician, specializing in Preventive Medicine. My medical education and experience encompass work and training in Internal Medicine, Emergency Medicine, Occupational and Urgent Care Medicine, Preventive Medicine, and more. With the goal of preventing human suffering, I ultimately specialized and became certified in General Preventive medicine - concentrating on chronic diseases.

There are several levels of Preventive Medicine, including Primary, Secondary, and Tertiary Prevention.

Level 1 or Primary Prevention: Public education and implementation of hygienic principles are provided such as
- Optimal Diet and Exercise/Activity
- Intact Sewage Systems and Clean Water Supplies
- No Tobacco and Limited Alcohol use
- Sleep hygiene
- Sexual Hygiene

These actions can prevent disease in the first place.

Level 2 or Secondary Prevention: Medical screenings via medical and lifestyle histories, physical examinations, and lab tests are used to detect and diagnose problems that may be unknown because they may often have no apparent clinical manifestations initially:
- Hypertension, Pre-Diabetes, and Diabetes
- High Cholesterol and Abnormal Body Composition
- Precancerous PAP Test or Precancer of the Prostate or Breast

- History of dangerous Sexual Activity

Level 2 Prevention and Reversal of pre-clinical maladies can stop the development of clinically apparent diseases such as coronary heart disease, stroke, uncontrolled diabetes, cancer, and sexually transmitted infections.

Level 3 or Tertiary Prevention: Nutrition Optimization, Lifestyle & Integrative Medicine, Detoxification of the body from toxic metals and organic (carbon-based) pollutants, herbal and other integrative/complementary therapies, various intravenous (IV) infusion therapies and judicious use of modern allopathic medicine are all used to prevent worsening of chronic medical conditions and if possible, to improve or reverse those conditions.

With Tertiary Prevention - Coronary Heart disease, Type 2 Diabetes, Severe Steroid-dependent Eczema, Sarcoidosis, Gangrene from diabetic-accelerated atherosclerosis, and many other chronic diseases have been improved and reversed at our preventive medical facility, **Advanced Clinics for Preventive Medicine,** for over three decades.

Correcting dietary mistakes and other unhealthy lifestyle habits has proven to be an essential cornerstone to successfully preventing, stabilizing, and often reversing many of the chronic diseases plaguing our planet today. This book will give you the scientific rationale and direction in successfully using Optimal Nutrition, along with Holistic & Preventive medicine to Prevent, Curtail, and Reverse many modern chronic maladies.

Dr. William Richardson, M.D., M.S.P.H.

THE SCIENCE OF OPTIMAL NUTRITION

Why is it important to understand human nutrition at this time? Because Dietary and Environmental mistakes are responsible for over 95% of the chronic disease epidemics sweeping the planet today. In the United States, other Western countries and increasingly in developing nations, people are suffering more and more from chronic diseases such as heart and artery diseases, hypertension, renal (kidney) failure, diabetes, obesity, cancer, and Alzheimer's disease. As a nation, we often eat suboptimal foods, suffer from environmental pollution, and are oftentimes under more stress than we can handle.

Consider the fact that our culture "promotes" chronic disease development so well that Asians and Africans, traditionally devoid of Western chronic diseases, often develop the same chronic diseases that the U.S. population suffers upon moving to the U.S. These immigrants have been decultured, meaning that their original lifestyles and cultures were supplanted with the foreign & less healthy Western (U.S.) culture. For example, Okinawans of Japan are known for having some of the longest, disability-free, life expectancies in the world. However, younger Okinawans living *near* American military bases in Japan have adopted the American fast-food culture and, subsequently, have Japan's highest rates of obesity, heart disease, and premature death. Similarly, when Okinawans, other Asians, and Africans migrate to America, and if they adopt American diets and lifestyles, their rates of chronic disease and longevity will soon match the American rates.

The area where humans and human civilization originally developed is in Sub-Saharan Africa. This development or evolution took millions of years. It is estimated that our species, Homosapien, has been on the planet for over 350,000 years. In that environment, there were plenty of natural foods available for consumption: yams, whole grains, legumes, fresh and organic fruits, vegetables, seeds, and nuts. There were no man-made refined foods or fast foods, and less significant amounts of animal products were consumed. We had plenty of natural - unprocessed foods straight from "nature": raw, organic, plant-based whole foods to eat. We were in our most natural environment: "The Garden of Eden." Nowadays, in the U.S. and other Westernized nations, we have very unhealthy foods presented to us 24/7 in advertisements on television, radio, and billboards, telling us to consume some of the most unhealthy "foods" that have ever existed on the planet.

What was the "original" human diet actually like? It would be similar to the chimpanzee diet since we share 99.4% of our genes with them: 50% fruit, 40% dark greens/other vegetables, and 10% nuts, seeds, and insects. Gorillas eat a similar diet of 50 to 60 pounds of food per day consisting of fruits, nuts, seeds, and 22 pounds of green vegetables. Large vegan animals, such as elephants, eat enough vegetation to produce one hundred pounds of feces per day, and the hippopotamus eats about 80 pounds of greens daily. On the other hand, carnivores, such as cats (lions, tigers, and cougars) and dogs (wolves) eat animal bodies. They are anatomically equipped to kill and eat their prey, fresh and raw, with no tools.

When we explore the anatomical differences between carnivore and herbivore mammals, we will see that our bodies were originally designed for plant-based nutrition. Please study **Table 1** below. Humans can be omnivores as an adaptation to food availability - not as a physical need. Chimpanzees, gorillas, and humans evolved in Sub-Saharan Africa where there was plenty of food available that could be consumed naturally and whole. Most traditional human diets are plant-based since humans have no physiological need to consume meat. Those consuming a more plant-based diet are in fact healthier than those who consume significant amounts of meat or meat products in their diet. Many human populations thrive on a plant-based diet with longer lives and less disease load than those who consume animal products.

Table 1 - REASONS WE'RE NOT BUILT TO EAT MEAT			
	CARNIVORES (Lions, Tigers & Bears)	**HERBIVORES** (Gorillas, Horses & Cows)	**HUMAN BEINGS**
TEETH	Pointed & sharp. Long canines to tear flesh.	Mostly flat and blunt to grind plant food.	Mostly flat molars to grind nuts, vegetables, fruits, and grains.
Mouths & Jaws	Larger, stronger, and wider to capture their prey, but can't move sideways to grind plant food.	Can't open wide - but they can move from side to side to grind plant food.	Can't open wide, but can move from side to side to grind nuts and vegetables. Saliva contains starch and enzymes.
Claws	Long and sharp claws to tear flesh.	No Claws.	No Claws - only fingers to pick vegetables & fruits
Bowel Wall	Smooth, to let meat move along quickly.	Full of pouches. Meat could get stuck and putrefy (rot).	Full of pouches. Meat could get stuck and putrefy causing colon cancer and other problems.
Intestinal Track	Very short (3x body length); meat can pass through quickly without putrefying	Very long (12x body length); meat could putrefy.	Very long - meat could putrefy.
Stomach	Larger (65% of GI tract) to hold prey. Highly acidic to digest meat and ward off Bacteria.	Smaller (30% of GI tract) Very alkaline to digest carbohydrates easily.	Smaller (24% of GI tract) Very alkaline to digest carbohydrates easily.
Water Consumption	By lapping.	By sipping.	By sipping.
Instincts	When they see their prey bleeding, they pounce on it.	When they see smaller animals they don't yearn to kill them.	When most people see an injured, bleeding animal, they feel repulsed or want to help it.

There is plenty of anthropological evidence that ancestral human populations have traditionally followed a fiber-rich plant-based diet consisting mostly of fruits, vegetables, seeds, nuts, yams, whole grains and legumes (beans, peas & lentils). This diet helped prevent obesity[1] and chronic diseases such as type 2 diabetes,[2,3] heart and artery disease,[2,4,5,6] hypertension,[7] many cancers,[8] and more. Fortunately, paleontologists have studied the fossilized feces of early humans which they found consisted of digested plant-based foods, mostly vegetables, and fruits with very high fiber contents.[9] It has been proposed that the decline in fiber content of the diet in Westernized nations since the Industrial Revolution has played a major role in the current obesity epidemic.[10]

I first visited Africa in 1990 with my native-African friend, Manyo Ayuk. We traveled to various parts of Nigeria in West Africa as guests of his family for 21 days. During a visit to Manyo's home village, I met his 96-year-old father, Chief Osaji Ayuk - still very active with his life and family, including his six wives and 32 children. I was given a tour of the village by my friend's aunt. At 122 years old, she was walking at least 2 miles and gardening every day! The food in the village was fabulously delicious, nutritious, and over 96% plant-based, organic whole foods consisting of green vegetables, African yams in the form of Fufu, legumes, and various fruits, seeds & nuts. On the other hand, I also met with and counseled a younger woman who was set up to have stomach surgery because of chronic upper abdominal pain and indigestion that began after she started eating a more Westernized, meat-based, and processed foods diet. I also met a woman who was fighting obesity and type 2 diabetes. She was beginning to gain some success by cutting back on processed foods, walking more, and consuming more whole-natural foods. As a physician, I became concerned about suboptimal aspects of the Western culture encroaching on Africa, the motherland of all Humanity.

Add to those experiences, my conversations with many other native Africans regarding the healthy diets and lifestyles of their grandparents and great-grandparents. Unfortunately, some of the younger people in Africa have adopted less healthy lifestyles and diets as an effect of the colonization of Africa and subsequent Westernization of some of the Africans' diets and lifestyles.

In Atlanta, around the early 1990s, I met a younger African woman who had recently moved to America and suffered from hypertension, obesity, and past blood clots in her legs. I expressed my surprise that she had these medical problems. She stated that her grandparents and great-grandparents had none of those problems, and had essentially "perfect muscular bodies" of normal weight. She said that they ate great amounts of healthy, plant-based foods. They ate a very small amount of meat about twice a year as part of some ceremony. These elders were on no medications, had no chronic diseases, and often lived for well over 100 years in great health. She indicated that many of the current more Westernized members of her tribe (Zulu), who lived in large African cities, ate meat two to three times per day, were often on medications for chronic cardiovascular diseases such as hypertension, and stayed in and out of the hospitals.

Our large hospitals and medical centers, and enormous consumption of pharmaceuticals in the U.S. are testimonies to our failure in preventing chronic diseases. In 1900, the top killers in the United States were acute infectious diseases such as pneumonia, tuberculosis, and diarrheal diseases.[11] Currently, the top killers in the U.S. are chronic diseases such as coronary heart disease, cancer, stroke, and degenerative brain maladies such as Alzheimer's disease. The current epidemics of hypertension and diabetes heavily contribute to coronary heart disease, stroke, kidney failure, senility, and Alzheimer's disease. All of these chronic diseases are strongly related to the modern Western diet with its high amount of animal product consumption and refined food content

CASE STUDY: Too Young for a Migraine.

A 16-year-old male presented to a rural Georgian hospital emergency room one morning complaining of a migraine headache. I was the attending ER physician that day, taking care of all the patients coming in. The patient was being followed by and receiving care from Pediatric Headache Specialists in Atlanta, Georgia.

The patient had a pulsating headache that started the evening prior to the ER visit and had become moderately severe by the morning of admission to the ER. Besides the severe throbbing headache, the patient complained of nausea, light sensitivity (photophobia), sound sensitivity (sonophobia), along with neck and upper back muscle pain and tightness.

The lifestyle history revealed a diet that was fast food, junk food, and meat-based. He also suffered from severe chronic constipation, having a bowel movement about twice a month!

A physical exam revealed an obese teenage male in moderate distress. He had tenderness in the musculature of the neck (cervical muscles) and upper back (trapezius muscles). His nasal passages were blocked and he was mouth breathing.

I was appalled that the "Headache Specialists" had not educated the patient and his mother on the importance of optimal diet and lifestyle.

The patient received the following treatment that day in the ER:
- Intravenous(IV) hydration fluids.
- Anti-nausea injections through the IV line.
- Toradol shot for pain - an injectable nonsteroidal & non-narcotic anti-inflammatory medication: an ibuprofen(Motrin)-like drug.
- Ice packs to the head and neck.

- Osteopathic manipulations and trigger point massage.
- Extensive dietary and lifestyle counseling, emphasizing the necessity of a high fiber, plant-based diet to correct chronic constipation.

Results:
- The patient was relieved of his admitting complaints.
- The patient and his mother left the ER with enough information to self-treat and prevent further headaches.

Western physicians, who had set up and worked in a large system of missionary hospitals in Sub-Saharan Africa in the 1930s and 1940s, observed no chronic diseases such as heart and artery disease, hypertension, diabetes, nor obesity in the native Africans they were serving. On the other hand, those chronic diseases were devastating and killing members of the European and U.S. populations.[12] To illustrate these facts, let's analyze a study that was conducted in South Africa in 1994 by Dr. Dennis Burkitt, M.D. (a medical missionary) which compared the prevalence (number of cases in a population) of chronic diseases such as heart and artery disease, cancers, hypertension, obesity, type 2 diabetes, and others between the various population groups living in South Africa.[13] As observed in **Tables 2** and **3** that follow, the study demonstrated that heart disease and other chronic diseases, as well as top cancers found in the U.S. and other Western Industrialized nations such as lung, breast, colon, stomach, pancreatic, and prostate cancers, were unheard of in Rural Native African populations, who were less influenced by the "foreign" Westernized diet while the White South Africans had significantly much higher rates of heart disease, those five cancers, type 2 diabetes, hypertension, and strokes.

The data in **Table 4** demonstrate that, compared with Rural Black Native African populations, the White South Africans had significantly higher rates of noninfectious Gastrointestinal diseases such as hemorrhoids, appendicitis, Ulcerative Colitis, irritable bowel syndrome, diverticular disease, and colon cancer. Please refer to **Table 5** to compare the nutritional content of the Rural Native African diet versus the White South African and U.S. diets. Notice the change in dietary and disease patterns the more Westernized the various populations became. Rural Blacks are the least Westernized South African population, while White South Africans are the most Westernized. Notice the higher fat content of the U.S. populations in **Table 5.** The higher fat content of the U.S. Black population compared to the U.S. White population is likely secondary to the deculturation that Blacks underwent in the U.S.

DISEASE PATTERNS IN SOUTH AFRICAN POPULATIONS[13]

Table 2 - Frequencies of some Diseases of "Prosperity" in South African Populations

	Rural Blacks	Urban Blacks	Coloreds*	East Indians	Whites
Dental Caries	+	+	+++	++++	+++
Femoral Fractures	+	+	++	++	+++++
Obesity	+	+++	+++	+++	+++
Hypertension	+	++++	++++	+++++	+++++
Diabetes	+	+++	++++	+++++	+++++
Heart Disease	_a	+	++++	+++++	+++++
Stroke	+	++	+++	+++	++

Table 3 - Cancer Patterns in South African Populations

	Rural Blacks	Urban Blacks	Coloreds*	East Indians	Whites
Lung	_a	++	+++	++	++++
Breast	_a	++	+++	+++	+++++
Colon	_	+	++	++	+++++
Stomach	_	+	+++	+	++
Pancreas	_	+	++	+	+++
Cervix	++	++++	+++	+	+
Prostate	_	+	++	++	+++++

a--Implies that occurrence is rare; *--Implies racially mixed S. Africans

Table 4 - Frequencies of Noninfectious Bowel Diseases In South African Populations

	Rural Blacks	Urban Blacks	Coloreds*	East Indians	Whites
Hemorrhoids	–	++	++	++	+++
Appendicitis	+	++	++	++	+++++
Ulcerative Colitis	–	+	+	+	+++++
Irritable Bowel Syn.	–	++	++	+	++++
Diverticular Disease	–	+	++	++	+++++
Colon Cancer	–	+	++	++	+++++

Table 5 - Dietary Patterns in In South Africa and the U.S. Populations

	Rural Blacks	Urban Blacks	Coloreds*	East Indians	Whites
Energy from Fat (%)	7-15%	20-30%	30-35%	30-40%	35-50%
Carbohydrates (%)	70-75%	65-75%	60%	60%	55%
Dietary Fiber (grams)	20-25g	10-20g	15-20g	15-20g	15-20g

	U.S. Whites	U.S. Blacks
Energy from Fat (%)	40-50%	50-60%

From the book:
WESTERN DISEASES, Their Dietary Prevention and Reversibility[13]
By Dennis P. Burkitt M.D. and Norman J. Temples Ph.D

Let me reiterate: the two largest problems with the Modern Western diet are the consumption of refined food products and reliance on animal products. Consumption of animal products and the lack of fiber in consumed refined foods are causative agents in atherosclerotic heart and artery disease,[14] hypertension,[15] type 2 diabetes,[16] obesity,[17] cancer,[18] eczema and asthma,[19] other inflammatory disorders, middle ear infections,[20] and increased rates of neurodegenerative diseases such as Alzheimer's disease[21,22] and Parkinson's disease.[23] Animal products contain bio-accumulated pesticides and other fat-soluble environmental toxins in the fatty tissues of meat and the fat of animal products, such as cow's milk and cheese, in increasing concentrations with exposure to toxins in animal feed,[24] and from natural hormones in female animals, even grown organically. Among these environmental toxins include estrogen (female hormone) and estrogen-mimics (pesticides) which both contribute to increased rates of breast cancer,[25] precocious puberty in females,[26] decreased male potency,[27] gynecomastia (male breast development),[28] and feminization of the brain of the male fetus in-utero.[29] Indeed, a plant-based organic whole-food diet is optimal nutrition.

Most refined foods are plant-derived products made by removing protein, beneficial fats, minerals, trace elements, antioxidants, and fiber such as whole wheat berries being refined and ground into white flour. These products can be stored on the shelf for long periods of time because lower life forms such as bacteria, fungi, and insects don't gain nutritional benefits from feeding on refined foods as much as whole foods. The consumption of refined food products such as "foods" containing white flour, refined sugars, and high fructose corn syrup (HFCS) is much less satisfying to us because satiation is enhanced by the good fats, protein, and fiber that are removed in the refining process such that larger amounts tend to be eaten. Also, refined carbohydrates such as sugar, HFCS, and refined grains all cause abnormally high spikes in insulin hormone secretions from our pancreas in response to the high blood sugar levels that refined foods trigger. Insulin regulates our blood sugar levels by pushing glucose (sugar) into our cells. Chronic insulin elevation causes insulin resistance in the cells of our bodies, which is an underlying cause of the obesity and type 2 diabetes epidemics sweeping the U.S. and world today.

OPTIMAL NUTRITION:
Delicious Plant-Based Whole Foods

Let's explore the role that a plant-based diet, particularly rich in beneficial nutrients, may play in helping to prevent, arrest, and even reverse our leading causes of death and disability. At our clinic, the Advanced Clinics for Preventive Medicine, we have observed the reversal of many chronic medical conditions such as coronary heart disease, hypertension, type 2 diabetes, diabetic foot ulcers, gangrene, fibromyalgia, obesity, Sarcoidosis, and more. These diseases were reversed with no surgery, no miracle drugs, but by a plant-based whole foods dietary regimen along with other pertinent lifestyle changes, optimizing the structure and function of the body's organs and systems, and avoidance and detoxification of environmental toxins from the body.

We can optimize the nutritional intake of ourselves, our families, and eventually society-at-large. Where do we start? First, ponder this question: How did the first people on the planet survive in Sub-Saharan Africa? I don't think they were chasing and running down a cow to kill with their bare hands or eating them alive and raw as carnivores do such as non-domesticated lions, tigers, and wolves (or like the zombies of the Walking Dead television series). Rather, the first members of our species found themselves in tropical and semi-tropical forests with an abundance of fresh, colorful and tasty fruits, vegetables, fresh sprouts, legumes, seeds and nuts, whole grain plants, and tubers - such as yams. Did you know studies have demonstrated that ancestral humans of the past ate 100 grams of fiber daily, while modern, non-Westernized (usually more rural) African and Asian populations eat about 25 to 55 grams of fiber daily? Western industrialized humans barely consume 15 to 20 grams of fiber daily.[30] Fiber is exclusively contained in whole plant-based foods; while there is no fiber in animal products, period. The fiber contained in whole plant-based foods is associated with lower rates of the following: obesity,[31] type 2 diabetes,[32] heart and artery disease,[33] cancers of the breast[34] and colon,[35] hypertension,[36] strokes,[37] premature death in general,[38] and many other maladies. We will explore optimal human nutrition based on the best available evidence.

There is significant anthropological evidence that early humans throughout history have mainly consumed whole plant-derived foods. For example, a study published in 2009 produced evidence that humans living along the eastern coast of southern Africa (now Mozambique) consumed a diet based on the ancient cereal grain, sorghum, starting at least 105,000 years ago.[39] It has been documented that plants with underground complex carbohydrate storage organs or bulbs such as potatoes, and corms such as taro were major energy sources for Africans 30,000 years ago.[40] An archeological site in Israel, dating back about 23,000 years ago, had grass seeds and "oak acorns, almonds, pistachios, wild olives, and fruits and berries such as Christ's thorn, raspberry, wild fig, and wild grape."[41] A wide variety of plants have been a major feature of what early humans ate way before the dawn of agriculture.

CASE STUDY: "Can You Save My Foot?"

A middle-aged female with a history of type 2 diabetes presented to our clinic with gangrene on her 1st and 2nd toes of her foot. Gangrene is a type of tissue death caused by a lack of blood supply and infection. Symptoms usually include a change in skin color to red or black, swelling, pain, skin breakdown, and coolness. Surgeons were planning to amputate her affected foot in about 2 to 3 weeks. She'd had diabetes for about 8 years and stated that her diabetic mother passed away a few weeks after her foot had been amputated. This family history prompted the patient to seek an alternative to amputation.

Her diet was meat-based and full of refined foods reflected by high blood sugar levels in her bloodwork. She was moderately obese. Physical examination revealed her affected lower extremity with swelling, warmth, and a mottled red appearance from her knee down through her foot. The first and second toes of her affected foot were gangrenous with the characteristic green-black color. In other words, her toes were rotting off. She asked me, "Can you save my foot?" I told her that we would do our best. Diabetics are prone to gangrene of the lower extremities because of the accelerated atherosclerosis (hardening of the arteries) they get that decreases blood flow to the extremities.

The patient was placed on a whole food, plant-based dietary regimen - emphasizing plenty of green vegetables, legumes, whole grains, less-sweet fruit, and raw nuts & seeds. We consulted with an Infectious Disease specialist for appropriate oral antibiotics, which were instituted. The patient was given a number of relevant nutritional supplements including essential vitamins, minerals, trace elements, and antioxidants such as alpha lipoic acid - an important supplement for diabetics. She underwent IV Mg-EDTA chelation therapy for 30 treatments to reverse the atherosclerosis blocking her arteries, including those supplying her lower extremities(feet). Chelation therapy has been shown to work incredibly well in diabetics for reversing atherosclerosis. Also, we designed an amplified pyramid device that has been shown to slow down the growth of lower life forms(bacteria and mold) that she slept with over her affected foot.

    The results were profound. The infection and gangrene completely reversed. Her blood sugars were under control while she lost body fat. The gangrene never returned.

What does an optimal diet look like? An optimal diet is full of colorful, non-refined, and high fiber, plant-based foods. The ability to see colors in the animal kingdom is unique to humans, other primates, fish, amphibians, some reptiles, some birds, and bees & butterflies. Humans and other primates developed the ability to detect and are attracted to the blue-violet, green, yellow, orange, and red-colored natural antioxidant phytonutrients (plant nutrients) contained in fresh fruits and vegetables. These natural antioxidants quell free radicals which are unstable, violently reactive molecules that can damage our cellular structures, including genetic material in our DNA - and can cause early aging, fatigue, and cancer. Free radicals are formed as by-products of metabolic processes (regular chemical reactions in our bodies). Free radical formation in our bodies is accelerated by fat-soluble environmental pollutants such as pesticides which are bio-accumulated in the fats of animals consumed for food. Examples of the colorful antioxidants include the red lycopene phytonutrient in tomatoes, strawberries, and watermelons; the yellow and orange carotenoids in green leafy vegetables, sweet potatoes, and carrots; and the blue and purple anthocyanins in blueberries, plums, purple & black grapes, purple muscadines, and purple sweet potatoes. Consuming these antioxidant-containing foods enhances our survival and combats diverse conditions from viral infections, cancer, and heart disease to helping to preserve brain health.[42]

Plant-based foods contain no cholesterol and when sticking to a plant-based, whole foods diet, it's much easier to avoid saturated and trans fats which cause heart and artery disease. Since we evolved on an essentially plant-based diet, our bodies naturally manufacture all of the cholesterol we need as a precursor for many of our hormones, vitamin D, and more. Consuming meats such as fish, pork, poultry, and beef has also been linked to gout,[43] kidney failure,[44] and kidney stones[45] in addition to all of the maladies mentioned earlier.

The longer meat is cooked at higher temperatures, especially chicken, the more chemical substances are produced from muscle tissues called heterocyclic amines (HCA) which are associated with increased risks of cancers of the breast, colon, esophagus, lung, pancreas, prostate, and stomach.[46] Colorectal cancer has been repeatedly linked to low-fiber diets that are high in animal protein, fat, and refined carbohydrates.[47] A study found that those eating strictly plant-based diets (vegans) are three times more likely to have daily bowel movements, thereby pushing out the toxins that cause colorectal cancer.[48] Food travels through the vegan's GI (gastrointestinal) tract in one or two days. The transit time through the GI tract of individuals consuming a conventional meat-containing diet may take as long as five or more days. The bowel regularity of vegans protects them from many Western diseases as demonstrated in numerous studies.

The consumption of fat from animal sources, including meats, dairy products, and eggs was correlated with increased pancreatic cancer risk, while there was no such correlation found with the consumption of plant-based fat-containing foods such as nuts, seeds, avocados, and olive oil.[49]

What about cow's milk? Does it really do a body good? While all foods of animal origin contain sex hormones, such as estrogen (female sex hormone), today's genetically "improved" dairy (milk-producing) cows are presently milked throughout their pregnancies when their reproductive hormones are naturally even higher.[50] The human consumption of these hormones, which are naturally found in organic cow's milk as well, has been linked to the medical problems of hormone-related disorders such as acne,[51] diminished human male reproductive potency[52,] and precocious female puberty.[53] National population studies in Japan have revealed a twenty-five-fold increase of prostate cancer in Japanese men since World War II! This has coincided with the Westernization of the Japanese diet: a twenty-fold increase in dairy product consumption, a nine-fold increase in meat consumption, and a seven-fold increase in egg consumption.[54]

Did you know that male erectile dysfunction (ED) and our number one killer in the United States, coronary artery disease, are just two manifestations of the same disease of systemic (all over the body), inflamed, clogged, and damaged arteries (atherosclerosis), no matter which organs are afflicted.[55] While the United States has less than five percent of the world's total population of men, the United States has almost a third of the world's total impotent male population. Over 30 million men in the U.S. have ED out of the approximately one hundred million men with ED worldwide.[56] In men under forty years old, ED is often an early sign of generalized vascular disease. Young men with high cholesterol levels are at risk for future ED,[57] and then heart attacks and strokes later on as well as a shorter life span.[58] All of this is linked to a diet with high amounts of animal products and refined foods.[59] I guess that throws out the false notion that meat consumption is a "manly" thing to do.

Pistachio nuts to the rescue! A study demonstrated that when men with ED added three to four handfuls of pistachios a day to their diet for three weeks, they experienced a significantly stronger blood flow through the penis which resulted in significant improvements in erectile function (firmer erections) with no side effects.[60] Remember, whole foods such as nuts satiate us and decrease our intake of less desirable foods such as animal products and refined foods while providing healthy fats, fiber, and protein. Women with higher cholesterol levels may eventually experience female sexual dysfunction manifested by decreased arousal and lubrication, lower orgasm rates, and overall decreased sexual satisfaction. Female sexual dysfunction is caused by atherosclerosis of the pelvic arteries.[61] The Harvard Nurses' Health Study demonstrated an extension of a woman's life by eating two handfuls of nuts weekly. Therefore, eating healthier may extend your life as well as improve your love life.

CASE STUDY: "I want my life back from prostate cancer!"

A 70-year-old male presented to our clinic with prostate cancer that had spread(metastasized) extensively to his bones. He complained of severe, unrelenting bone pain, necessitating strong narcotic medications. Prostate cancer is often detected and assessed over time by measurements of a chemical that is released into the blood by the prostate gland called the prostate-specific antigen(PSA). Normal PSA levels detected in the blood usually range from 0 to 4 ng/mL. An optimal level is 2.5 to 3 and lower. His PSA level was 2,500 ng/mL! This is considered an extremely high and alarming level and was the highest PSA level that I had ever encountered at that time. I agreed to institute the best program possible in order to help this patient.

Our patient received dietary and lifestyle counseling and as a result changed his diet to a plant-based whole food diet. He consumed lots of raw greens in salads and raw vegetable-based smoothies. He quit all animal and refined food products. We gave him a regimen of high potency dietary supplements, high dose vitamin C intravenously, Haelan platinum fermented soy beverage, and other pertinent supplements and herbals.

These were the results:
- PSA levels decreased to 13.6 ng/mL (from 2,500)!
- The pain subsided and the patient was able to stop all narcotic pain medications.
- He took his wife to Las Vegas (twice) and other vacation spots within the next year.
- He lived another seventeen (17) years with no recurrence of cancer, passing of natural causes.

The evidence points us away from animal and refined food products as optimal human nutrition. But, what about getting enough protein? The whole foods plant-based diet supplies all the protein we will ever need from legumes (beans), whole grains, starchy vegetables, nuts, seeds, and dark green vegetables. Broccoli contains more protein per calorie than steak and, per calorie, spinach is about equal to chicken and fish. Remember, elephants eat enough vegetables to make one hundred pounds of feces per day and gorillas eat fifty to sixty pounds of food daily, including twenty-two pounds of greens but, generally, no meat except a few insects. Their large bone & muscle masses are well maintained by plant-based diets. Eating a variety of vegetables, legumes, whole grains, fruits, seeds, and nuts to satisfaction will supply us with the protein and calcium we need to thrive.

A diet centered around whole plant foods not only prevents and reverses heart and artery diseases but is the safest diet for healthy weight loss. Eating a fiber-rich, plant-based whole foods diet will satisfy your hunger, and allow you to eat more food, while still losing weight. The side effects are normalization of cholesterol, blood pressure, and sugar levels, improved bowel function, clearer skin, and a better sex life.

Plant-based diets can improve your health, head to toe. Whole food plant-based diets can lower blood pressure and cholesterol, and decrease your chance of heart attacks, cancer, arthritis, kidney disease, and diabetes. Women can experience less menstrual pain, fibroids, endometriosis, infertility, and few menopausal symptoms. You can get better sleep, have more energy, have smoother skin, and longer life. Remember, the same recommendations for reducing our nation's top killer, cardiovascular disease can improve COVID-19 and other infectious disease outcomes.

Plant-based diets even make the planet healthier! That's because the same foods that are good for your health are good for the planet.

Vegetarian protein sources, such as lentils, black beans, chickpeas, and tofu are minimal contributors to greenhouse gas emissions while beef, cheese, and other animal products are very large contributors. The health of the planet is dependent on our food choices!

HEALTHY PRINCIPLES TO LIVE BY

1. On a day-to-day basis, consume a diet of organic plant-based whole food nutrition. Whole food starches such as whole grains, sweet potatoes, and legumes should be our primary energy sources. Include generous portions of vegetables and fruits. The more plant-based whole foods and the fewer refined & processed foods and animal products, the better.[62]

2. Making sensible food choices for yourself and your family benefits you all in the long run with better health and wellbeing. Examples include the decisions: to avoid meat, dairy products, eggs, and added sugar entirely; to consume only whole grains - not refined grains, and to never prepare or cook food with oil (a refined food product).

3. Decide not to have junk food present in the house. When you get hungry, you can eat a crisp, organic, red delicious apple or another fruit, and a few raw nuts or a wholesome vegan snack, such as Nanna's snack packs.

4. Choose more colorful foods over white or beige-colored foods: The deeper colored foods have significantly more phytonutrient antioxidants.
   Examples:
   - Choose Red Onions over Yellow Onions, and Yellow Onions over White Onions.
   - Choose Yellow Corn over White Corn.
   - Choose Yellow peaches over White Peaches.
   - Choose Purple Grapes over Green Grapes.
   - Choose Kale over Dark Lettuce, and Dark Lettuce over Iceberg Lettuce.

5. Choose to consume organic and locally grown foods whenever possible. Shop at Farmers Markets, Health Food Stores, and Grocery Stores with Organic Produce and Health Food Sections. "Even better, grow your own vegetables."

6. **Consider the following Recipe Conversions for Optimal Nutrition:**

    ❖ **Choose three of your favorite meals that you enjoy that are nearly plant-based and convert them to fully plant-based whole food meals.**

    ➢ **Examples:**
      - **Pasta and marinara sauce:** Change to whole-grain pasta with added vegetables (broccoli, cabbage, carrots, and onions) to the marinara sauce; sprinkle with chopped, raw walnuts.
      - **Stir-fried vegetables on rice:** Change to whole-grain, brown or red rice; Saute organic vegetables (broccoli, carrots, Bok-choy, and red onions) with precooked legumes (black beans, kidney beans, or garbanzo beans) in veggie-broth stock (no oil), flavored with herbal seasonings.
      - **Bean soup and French fries:** Change to vegan (containing no animal products) bean soup with chopped vegetables and baked sweet potatoes.

    ❖ **Choose three meals that you and your family already eat that contain meat (flesh of any animal), animal products (dairy and eggs), or refined food products, and replace them with plant-based whole food ingredients.**

➤ **Examples:**

- **Bean chili with vegetables:** Change beef chili and white bread to bean chili with vegetables and a green salad with sprouted whole grain bread (try Ezekiel sprouted whole-grain bread - in the frozen section of health food stores and health food frozen sections in grocery stores).

- **Veggie-burger with baked sweet potato "fries":** Change hamburger meat on a white bun and typical French fries to veggie-burger (homemade or a commercial vegan burger) on a sprouted whole grain bun and <u>baked</u> or <u>air fried</u> sweet potato "fries."

- **Healthy Super Salad:** Change a typical club salad with ham, cheese, and turkey on iceberg lettuce to a Super Salad with dark green, leafy lettuce with chopped broccoli, shredded sweet potatoes, diced avocado, finely shredded purple cabbage, thinly sliced red onions with pumpkin seeds and blueberries with a no-oil Tahini Lemon dressing (see **RECIPES**).

CASE STUDY: "Write more prescriptions!"

Did you know that drug company representatives, often called "drug reps", actually track how many prescriptions are written by the doctors they service? I didn't realize that until a drug rep, who had suggested that I prescribe the steroid nasal inhaler made by her company, asked me why I prescribed the inhaler only once per patient while all the other doctors she serviced continued to prescribe the inhaler to their patients month after month.

Steroid nasal inhalers are usually prescribed to reduce nasal and sinus inflammation, congestion, mucus production, and nasal swelling. Those annoying symptoms are caused by such conditions as allergic rhinitis, hay fever, dust exposure, and more. Nasal steroids are most often prescribed for persistent inflammation of the nose aka chronic rhinitis. Apparently, most physicians consider these steroid nasal inhalers to be "the solution."

Generally, appropriate reasons to prescribe pharmaceutical medications are for emergency situations, to get the ball rolling in the treatment of serious diseases such as heart disease, or as a necessity for certain acute or chronic medical problems that are resistant to more natural healing approaches such as trauma, or serious infections. When working in emergency rooms, I've had to prescribe and order medications for heart attacks, acute appendicitis, painful migraine headaches, severe infections, serious trauma, and much more. The treatment of chronic rhinitis may initially be treated with a steroid inhaler but can usually be solved by natural approaches.

Chronic sinusitis should be approached with dietary and environmental solutions. Over the years, I've found that dietary optimization can aid in decreasing the mucus production and thickness in the upper respiratory tract (nose and sinuses) and lower respiratory tract (windpipe and lungs).

Years ago, when I was attending medical school, I personally used to suffer from chronic rhinitis and sinusitis until I eliminated dairy products from my diet and detoxified my body. At the same time, I increased my intake of fresh fruits and vegetables, used hot peppermint tea, and drank plenty of clear fluids. The decrease in my symptoms was dramatic and has been reproduced in many of our patients over the years.

In our practice, we have cleared up chronic rhinitis, time and time again, usually without the use of any medication.

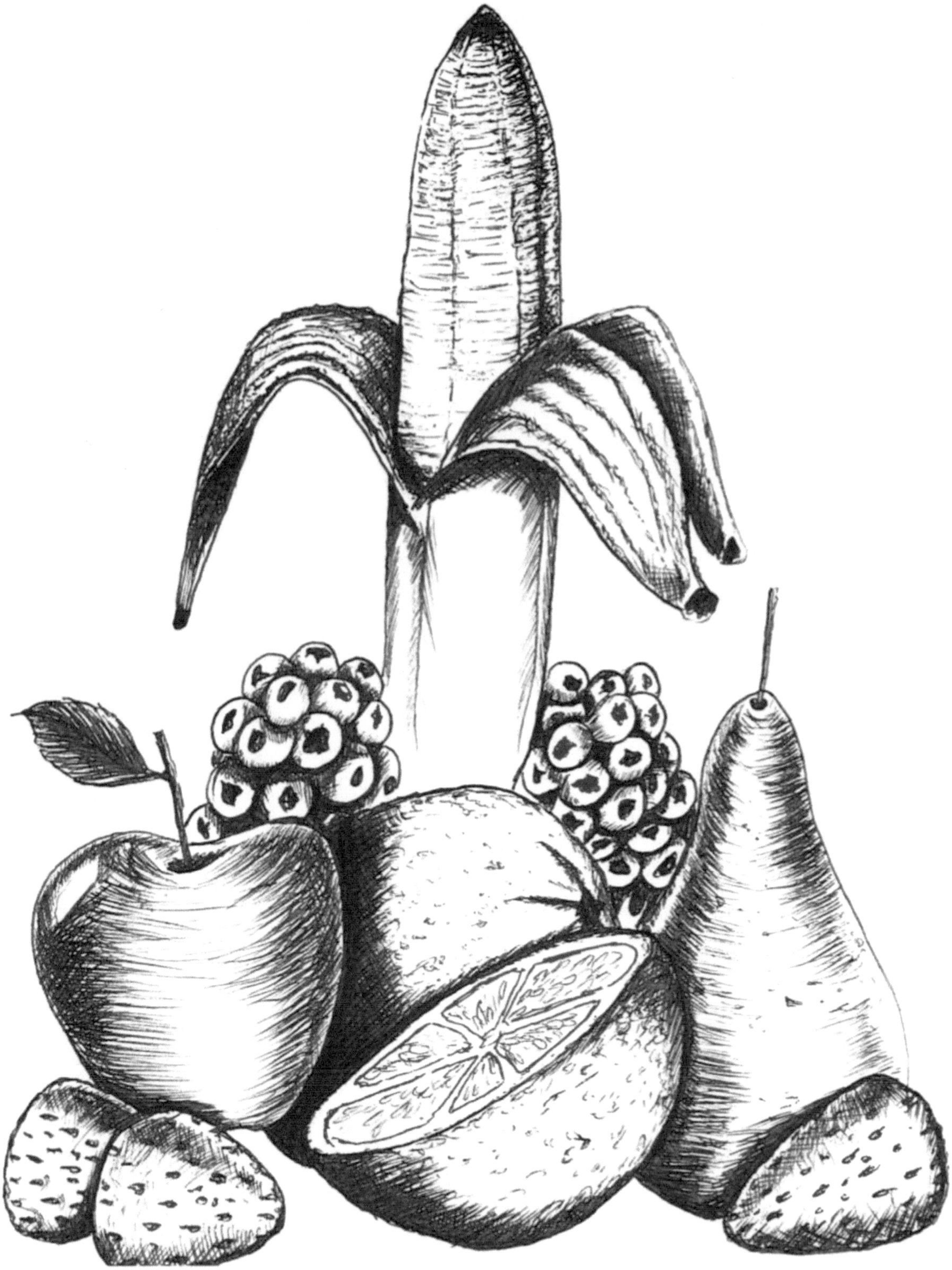

NUTRIENT SOURCES IN VEGAN CUISINE

VEGAN ENERGY SOURCES

Our primary source of energy is from starch containing foods such as grains, legumes, and starchy vegetables. These foods contain energy storage substances called starches, made up of long, often branched chains of sugar molecules or carbohydrates that we have enzymes to digest (break down) into individual sugar molecules for easy absorption into our bodies across the intestinal wall. Carbohydrates are made up of carbon, hydrogen, and oxygen atoms similar to wood. Fire burns wood in the presence of oxygen to produce energy in the form of heat and light, releasing carbon dioxide (CO_2). Similarly, our bodies need oxygen to produce energy from the starch-containing foods we eat to sustain us, and we exhale CO_2. Our bodies must constantly have energy to maintain life. Fires cease with no fuel.

Fiber is also made up of chains of sugar carbohydrates, but in a different way. We do not have the enzymes to digest and break fiber apart into individual sugar molecules for absorption. Termites and cows masticate or chew wood and hay to mechanically break the fiber down, and the bacteria in their digestive tracts produce the enzymes to further break down the fiber into individual sugar molecules that are absorbed across their GI tracts into their bodies to be used for their energy needs. We will discuss the benefits and necessity of the undigested fiber in our GI tract in an upcoming section.

We can derive energy from fruit as well, however fruits contain more simple sugar molecules that are not in chains and therefore quickly absorbed and used up, leaving us wanting more to avoid hunger. Other primates such as chimpanzees and gorillas derive significant amounts of their energy from fruit and must be constantly eating. Humans have 300% to 400% more starch digesting enzymes than other primates, allowing us to derive energy from starchy vegetables, legumes, and grains.

Whole grains, legumes, and starchy vegetables are the major foods for our energy needs. They should consist of about 65 - 70% of our diet to as low as 50%, if trying to release excess body fat.

WHOLE GRAINS: Amaranth, barley, buckwheat, bulgur, corn, farro, kamut, kaniwa, millet, oats, quinoa, rice, rye, sorghum, spelt, teff, wheat, and wild rice.

LEGUMES: Adzuki, black, cannellini, chickpeas also called garbanzo, cranberry beans, edamame, great northern, green peas, lentils, lima, kidney, mung, and navy.

STARCHY VEGETABLES: Artichokes, boniato (Caribbean sweet potato), carrots, parsnips, potatoes, salsify, sweet potatoes, winter squashes (acorn, butternut, hubbard, kabocha spaghetti), and yams (including African yam & Fufu).

Many starchy vegetables can be soaked & sprouted, fermented raw, processed raw, or cooked.

VEGAN PROTEIN SOURCES

Protein resides in abundance in the following list of plant-based whole food groups. Remember that creating meals that combine foods from several different food groups increases the value of the meal, but it's not strictly necessary to combine vegan protein-containing foods at every meal. Below, are listed the 9 essential amino acid building blocks of protein not manufactured by the body that must be consumed. If enough plant-based foods - especially: starchy vegetables, legumes, and whole grains - containing essential amino acids are consumed over the course of the day, there should not be any concern for protein deficiency.

- **WHOLE GRAINS:** The best choices within this group are "dinner grains" such as brown rice, millet, quinoa, barley, corn, etc., and also whole grain cereals, pasta, and bread. Try combination dishes such as millet casseroles, sauteed veggies over brown rice, whole-grain lasagna & spaghetti. Ezekiel brand sprouted products are excellent sources of whole grains.

- **LEGUMES:** The entire bean family (black, kidney, lima, organic soybean, pea, black-eyed, lentil, etc.) are great sources of energy and protein. Consider including the versatile organic soybean products like sprouted organic tofu or tempeh in tofu sandwich spreads or cutlets, and tofu omelets. Try beans, tofu or tempeh mixed into spaghetti sauce or veggie and grain casseroles. All sprouts (alfalfa, soy, mung, lentil, chickpea, sunflower, etc.) can be served in salads. Garbanzo beans, black beans, or lentils, sprouted or cooked, can be blended and made into spreads like "hummus."

- **STARCHY AND GREEN LEAFY VEGETABLES:** Starchy energy containing foods such as sweet potatoes (shredded or baked) & corn - served raw in salads or lightly steamed, legumes - such as lentil or bean soup, or baked red rice, brown rice, or quinoa are excellent protein sources. Broccoli, spinach, kale, bok choy, collards, beet tops, mustard greens, and other green vegetables contain protein. Remember, Gorillas consume about 22 pounds of green vegetables daily.

Consuming adequate volumes of starchy vegetables, legumes and whole grains to satisfy your energy needs and healthy appetite will ensure adequate protein intake.

- **SEEDS & NUTS:** Sunflower seeds, pumpkin seeds, sesame seeds (tahini), peanuts, almonds, walnuts, cashews, filberts, Brazils, macadamias, pistachios; in salads, dinner meals like sautes; nut-butters on whole-grain bread for sandwiches; with breakfast cereals, fruit bowls, deserts, etc. Nuts and seeds should be eaten in their raw state only, and in limited amounts compared to other less fatty vegan protein sources.

COMPLETE VEGAN PROTEIN: Amino acids are the building blocks of protein. There are 20 amino acids that we use in making our human proteins: we can manufacture 11 amino acids within our cells, while 9 "essential" amino acids have to be obtained from our dietary intake. These 9 essential amino acids generally have to be consumed daily.

The 9 essential amino acids are:		
Methionine	Phenylalanine	Threonine
Lysine(lower in grains, except buckwheat; higher in legumes)		
Tryptophan	Valine	Leucine
Histidine(essential up to 6 months of age)		
Isoleucine		

You do not need to consume animals & animal products to have enough protein in your diet. **Solely consuming plant-sourced proteins can provide enough of both the essential and non-essential amino acids - as long as the caloric intake is high enough to meet your energy needs.** You will know you have consumed enough whole plant-based food to meet your energy needs when your healthy appetite is satisfied. **It may help if the dietary sources of the plant-based protein are varied.**

Whole grains, legumes, vegetables, and nuts & seeds all contain both essential and non-essential amino acids and will supply all of the protein you will need. **Although, you won't need to consciously combine whole plant-based foods within a particular meal, it is wise to eat a variety of those vegan foods containing protein, various vitamins & minerals during each day and even within each meal to maximize nutritional quality.**

Sound vegan protein food source examples include: Quinoa, Buckwheat noodles, Organic Tofu - Tempeh - edamame, Amaranth, Ezekiel bread, Hemp seeds, Chia seeds, Brown rice and beans, Whole grain pita with hummus, Lima beans with broccoli & carrots, Chickpeas with mustard greens, and on and on.

<u>Red meat, poultry, fish, and animal products such as eggs and dairy products contain plenty of acid-producing sulfur-containing amino acids which produce detrimental amounts of acid in the blood</u>. This excess acid is buffered by calcium derived from our bones. This is why animal & animal product consumption is the major risk factor for osteoporosis and kidney stones. Also, Dr. John McDougall in his book, **The Starch Solution**, reveals that the sulfur-containing amino acids consumed from eating meats and animal products produce the "rotten eggs" odor causing "bad breath, body odor, and foul-smelling gas and stools."[63]

VEGAN VITAMIN & MINERAL SOURCES

Similar to essential amino acids, our bodies are not designed to manufacture essential vitamins. Except for vitamin B12 and vitamin D, plants manufacture the vitamins we need.

For healthy cell metabolism as well as proper blood, nerve & muscle function, your body needs to obtain 2 "families" of essential vitamins from the diet as follows:

- Those that dissolve in water **(water-soluble)**.
- Those that dissolve in oil **(fat-soluble)**.

WATER-SOLUBLE VITAMINS

WATER-SOLUBLE VITAMINS are not stored in the body and must, therefore, be supplied daily. They include B vitamins and vitamin C:

"B-COMPLEX" VITAMINS	
B-1 (Thiamine)	Pantothenic Acid
B-2 (Riboflavin)	Folic Acid
B-6 (Pyridoxine)	Niacin
Biotin	Choline (not essential)
see special note "below" on B-12	

A plentiful supply of the **B-Vitamins** can be obtained by daily consumption of a good variety of food types which include: **Green Leafy Veggies, Whole Grains, Legumes & Nutritional Yeast.**

The other water soluble vitamin is Vitamin C. Vitamin C is found in **Fruits such as Melons, Citrus (Oranges, Grapefruit, and Lemons), Bell Peppers, Tomatoes, and Berries.**

Also, Vitamin C is found in the following Veggies:

GREEN VEGGIES that contain Vitamin C		
Alfalfa Sprouts	Collards	Romaine Lettuce
Asparagus	Endive	Spinach
Green Beans	Kale	Broccoli
Leaf Lettuce	Bok Choy	Leeks
Brussel Sprouts	Mustard Greens	Cabbage Family
Parsley	Sprouts (mung, lentil. Sunflower, etc.)	

FAT-SOLUBLE VITAMINS

FAT-SOLUBLE VITAMINS are able to be stored in the body (notably, in the liver), and are needed in the diet "at least" 3 to 5 times per week.
They include:
        Vitamin A   Vitamin K   Vitamin E   Vitamin D

Vitamin A is made in the body from **provitamin-A** (beta-carotene and many other carotenoids) abundantly supplied by **Yellow Veggies,** especially: **Carrots, Corn, Pumpkin, Sweet Potato, Rutabaga,** as well as **Squashes** including **Acorn, Butternut, Hubbard, Spaghetti, Summer,** etc.

Provitamin-A carotenoids are also contained in **Yellow Fruits** such as **Apricots, Peaches & Mangoes** ....as well as **Tomatoes**. And perhaps surprisingly--**Green Leafy Veggies** are also some of the richest sources of **provitamin-A** such as those in the table above, **Green Veggies** that contain **Vitamin C.**

It is important to **obtain plenty of carotenoids in the diet** because some individuals may have a more sluggish conversion of carotenoids to the active form of vitamin A due to genetic variations, gut microbial health(take probiotics after antibiotic use), heavy alcohol use, and one's overall state of health. If there is some concern, vitamin A levels can be measured and if low, supplemented with up to 1500mcg(5,000 units) of vitamin A, daily.

Vitamin E & Essential Fatty Acids are found in:
- **Nuts and Seeds** - **Almonds, Peanuts, Sunflower Seeds, Flax Seeds, Sesame Seeds, etc.**
- **Seaweeds** - **Wakame, Nori, Irish Moss** and **Seaweed oil**

Vitamin K is obtained through eating **Green Leafy Veggies**.

Vitamin D is a nutrient that is ideally obtained from **exposing your skin (at least the face and forearms) to the Sun:** a minimum of 30 minutes for more melanated people under 60 years old and 1 hour for melanated people 60 years and older, while less melanated people under 60 years old need at least 15 minutes of solar exposure and 30 minutes for those 60 years and older.

Vegan food sources of **Vitamin D** include: Maitake and Portabella Mushrooms as well as vitamin D fortified vegan foods such as Cereals and Plant-based milks.

Vitamin D supplementation may be very helpful for strict vegans that are not able to get adequate daily exposure to direct Sunlight - especially in colder months:

- If very deficient, adults may need to supplement up to 5000-10,000 IU vitamin D per day, 5 days/week until normal blood levels are reached. Vitamin D supplements should contain or be taken with 100-150 mcg of Vitamin K2.
- Maintenance daily doses are up to 2000 to 4000 IU daily for 9 years old and up. **Levels may be measured via blood tests as necessary. Follow your physician's recommendations.**

Special note of Vitamin B-12:

Much unnecessary worry has been generated over "getting enough B-12." Vegans, seldom if ever, show signs of a B-12 deficiency. Vegans can obtain their **B-12** supply from yeast extracts (Nutritional Yeast), and fermented foods (sauerkraut, Kimchi, coconut yogurt, raw fermented pickle juice), as well as from **B-12** enriched or fortified foods such as plant-based milks (shake before serving) and cereals. Additionally, Healthy Gut Bacteria living in our intestines can provide some vitamin B-12. Early humans had obtained B12 from bacteria in their less than sterile environment. The B-12 in meat & animal products comes from the bacteria infecting and contaminating the meat & animal products.

Unlike other B Vitamins, **B-12** is stored in the body for long periods of time. However, because a B-12 deficiency (though unlikely with "proper" vegan nutrition) can be severe, and since vegans may not consume enough of the plant based **B-12** containing foods above, **<u>vegans should take B-12 supplements or multivitamins containing B-12 regularly:</u>** Take one 2,500 microgram (mcg) **B-12** tablet weekly, or 250mcg **B-12** daily. Consider crushing a few **B-12** tablets and adding the powder to gravies, smoothies, plant-based milk, salad dressings, etc. to make it convenient for an individual or the whole family.

While obtaining sufficient **B-12** should never be considered rationale for eating meat, dairy, or other harmful and unnecessary animal products - **getting enough vitamin B-12 is absolutely non-negotiable for vegans.**

VEGAN MINERAL SOURCES

CALCIUM: Green leafy vegetables: Kale, broccoli, collards; 1 cup of any of these greens, raw or cooked, has approximately the same content as a 6-oz. glass of cow's milk, without the troublesome phosphate load.	**IRON:** Dark green leafy veggies, whole grains, legumes, wheat germ, beets, barley, artichokes, beans, apricots & plums, and molasses/sorghum.
SELENIUM: Brazil nuts (2-3 per day), broccoli, cabbage, wheat germ, whole Grains, nutritional yeast.	**ZINC:** Kale, spinach, onions, mushrooms, soybeans, wheat germ, sunflower seeds, whole grains, nutritional yeast.

Animals obtain minerals from whole plant foods. Plants obtain minerals from the soil.

ESSENTIAL DIETARY FIBER

Filling your plate with **whole, plant-based foods** gives your body the fiber it needs to stay healthy. The indigestible parts of plant-based foods such as cellulose, lignin, and pectin are called, "dietary fiber." These substances are resistant to the action of digestive enzymes that break down non-fiber parts of food such as (non-fiber) carbohydrates, protein, and fats into elemental (small) parts: sugars, amino acids, and fatty acids which are readily absorbed through the intestinal wall for use in the body. We humans do not possess the specific enzymes that break down larger fiber molecules into its elemental parts. Therefore, fiber is not absorbed into the body from the intestines.

Fiber in vegetables, fruits, beans, and whole grains is important for optimal digestion and bowel regularity, weight management, blood sugar regulation, keeping cholesterol levels down, and more. Additionally, fiber is linked to longevity and decreased risk of cancer. Please refer to **Table 6**.

Table 6 - Fiber and Calorie Amounts in Various Foods

FIBER - grams/pound	FOOD	CALORIES/pound
19.9g	Vegetables	100
11g	Fruits	300
33.2g	Unrefined Carbohydrates*	500
22g	Legumes**	600
0	Fatty Protein Sources(Meat/Animal products)	650
0	Refined Carbohydrates***	1400
0	Sugar	1800
Little or none	Junk Food****	2300
30g	Nuts/Seeds	2800
0	Oils	4000

To acquire and maintain a healthy weight:

- Eat Vegetables, Fruits, Unrefined Carbohydrates, Legumes ad-lib (freely). The fiber in these lower calorie foods fills you up.
- Nuts/Seeds may be eaten sparingly in small amounts.

*such as oats, brown rice, and sweet potatoes.
**such as black beans, pinto beans, lentils, peas, and garbanzo beans.
***such as white rice, white flour products - white bread, and white spaghetti.
****unhealthy food that is high in calories from sugar or fat, with little dietary fiber, protein, vitamins, minerals, or other important forms of nutritional value.

Table 6 shows that plant-based whole foods are higher in fiber per Calorie content. Consuming higher fiber-containing foods will increase the quality or state of being fed or gratified to or beyond capacity - the definition of **satiety**. You will be more satisfied, healthier, and more easily maintain normal weight when you consume foods with higher fiber content: vegetables, fruits, unrefined grains, and legumes. Nuts and seeds are high in beneficial fiber, but should be consumed in moderation because of their higher calorie density. Calorie density is a measure of the calorie content of food relative to its weight or volume. It is also called energy density. We will store excess calories as fat in the body. Therefore, consuming higher calorie foods is associated with unwanted weight gain.

Fatty protein sources (meat/animal products), refined carbohydrates, sugar, and oils should be avoided because they have **no fiber content**, while having plenty of Calories. Junk foods have a high calorie density, and little or no fiber, and should be avoided as well.

There are two types of fiber: soluble and insoluble.

Both soluble and insoluble fiber have important and distinct benefits. Consuming adequate amounts of fiber helps us feel fuller on fewer calories and rids our system of excess hormones and toxins.

Most plant-based whole foods contain both soluble and insoluble fiber, but amounts of each vary in different foods. Remember, most or all fiber is removed from refined foods during processing: sugar cane to sugar; wheat berries to white flour. Soluble fiber dissolves in water (think of creamy oatmeal) forming a goo (a wet and sticky substance) that traps and holds toxins to be discharged from the body through the gastrointestinal (GI) tract. Insoluble fiber doesn't get gooey like oatmeal. Rather, it behaves like tiny little scrub brushes, keeping the intestinal contents moving along quickly out of the GI tract.

Roles of Soluble Fiber: decreasing blood sugar levels, lowering blood cholesterol levels, and facilitating the movement of excess estrogen and toxins (processed by the liver) out of the body through the bowels.

Good Sources of Soluble Fiber: oats, beans, lentils, peas, barley, vegetables, and some fruits including apples, citrus fruits, and berries.

Roles of Insoluble Fiber: acts like a broom, speeding up the passage of food through the digestive tract. It also increases fecal bulk, making stools easier to pass. All of this helps maintain regularity and prevents constipation.

Good Sources of Insoluble Fiber: whole grains such as brown rice, whole wheat & wheat berries, fruits including less sweet fruits such as tomatoes & cucumbers, vegetables such as greens, cauliflower & potatoes, beans, and lentils.

Some foods are good sources of both types of fiber including nuts and carrots.

How much Fiber should we consume each day? While most people in industrial nations like the United States get only 10 to 15 grams of fiber a day, **consuming at least 40 grams of fiber per day is recommended for healthy people.** Use the chart below to add up your daily fiber intake.

Use the **Check Your Fiber Chart** below to see how you can reach at least 40 grams of fiber per day in your own dietary intake.

CHECK YOUR FIBER CHART

Legumes	Serving Size	Calories	Fiber (grams)
Lentils, cooked	1 cup	230	11
Chickpeas, cooked	1 cup	270	12.4
Black beans, cooked	1 cup	228	15

Vegetables

Broccoli, cooked	1 cup	54	5
Sweet potato, baked, with skin	1 medium	105	3.8
Kale, cooked	1 cup	47	5.2
Kale, raw	1 cup	34	1.3

Fruits

Apple, with skin	1 small	77	3.6
Raspberries	½ cup	32	4
Banana	1 medium	105	3.1
Figs, dried	¼ cup	93	3.7

Grains

Quinoa, cooked	1 cup	222	5.2
Bulgur, cooked	1 cup	152	8.2
Oatmeal, cooked	1 cup	166	4
Brown rice, cooked	1 cup	215	3.5

Nuts and Seeds

Almonds	1 ounce	164	3.5
Chia seeds, dry	1 Tbsp	69	4.9
Pistachios	1 ounce	160	3

CASE STUDY: "I want to avoid my 4th open heart surgery!"

An 89 year old male Korean War Veteran first presented to my office in a wheelchair. Previously, he had endured three (3) open heart <u>c</u>oronary <u>a</u>rterial <u>b</u>ypass <u>g</u>raft (CABG) surgeries for narrowed or clogged up <u>coronary arteries</u> that <u>supply the heart muscle with oxygen and nutrients</u>. This disease is technically called atherosclerotic coronary heart disease. Atherosclerosis means "hardening" of the arteries and is manifested by the buildup of "plaque" - consisting of fats, cholesterol, inflammatory cells, and other substances in and on the inner artery walls. The arteries supplying the heart are called "coronary" arteries because they surround the heart just like a crown surrounds the head. This patient sought out our clinic as an alternative to receiving an expected 4th open heart surgery he desperately wanted to avoid.

CABG surgery involves an incision of the front (anterior) chest wall - where the front part of the rib cage, called the sternum, is split open with a saw. This procedure is called a thoracotomy. Once the chest wall is opened, metal retractors are used to hold the chest wall open to reveal the live beating heart. The ingoing and outgoing blood of the heart, traveling through the main arteries and veins of the heart, are rerouted through a Heart Lung Machine, which literally does the work of the heart and lungs. The heart is cooled and placed in a non beating, paralized state by a heart-paralyzing (cardioplegic) solution. Then, the cardiothoracic surgeon severs a breast artery or leg vein to be used to <u>bypass</u> the part of a coronary artery that is grossly clogged up from atherosclerotic (hardening of the arteries) plaque. No wonder why our client wanted to avoid CABG surgery.

Remember, the coronary arteries have the extremely important job of supplying the heart muscle with oxygen and nutrients. That's why atherosclerotic heart disease is so dangerous to have and must be addressed when detected. Typically, atherosclerotic heart disease is treated with medications and invasive procedures such as CABG surgery or balloon angioplasties, usually with stents.

Balloon angioplasty, which means molding of a blood vessel with a balloon, involves use of a very thin tube introduced into the narrowed, diseased portion of an atherosclerotic artery. Next, a balloon is opened up within the diseased artery to force the plaque up against the inner arterial wall to increase blood flow. Often, a stent (tubular support) is then placed inside the artery to hold the plaque up against the inner wall. Both CABG surgery and balloon angioplasties, with or without stent placements, are considered invasive procedures that carry serious potential risks and side effects.

The following quote was written on the black board on the first day of my Pharmacology class at Temple University, Lewis Katz School of Medicine (1975-1979):

"All Drugs are Poisons with Desirable Side Effects."

The patient was on seven(7) heart and hypertension (HTN) medications when he first presented to our preventive medicine facility. Some of his medications controlled symptoms of his heart disease which manifested as chest pain (called angina pectoris) that occurred when the patient exerted himself (walking or moving quickly). The clogged coronary arteries supplying the heart would not allow enough blood flow to supply adequate oxygen. Affected heart cells produce pain when deprived of oxygen. Some of his medications were used to control HTN.

Although the medications did control the HTN and chest pain, he had a very poor quality of life: mostly wheelchair bound, very low energy level, unable to exercise, poor appetite, and subsequent depression. These serious problems were a combination of medication side effects and effects from the heart disease.

Once drugs are prescribed, most patients are on them for life!

Most physicians fail to look for the true causes of chronic diseases such as coronary atherosclerotic heart disease, hypertension, diabetes, and obesity. Drugs are designed to block or disrupt aspects of the functioning biochemistry (chemistry of our bodies) causing an intentional imbalance in the body as an attempt to correct abnormal biochemical effects of disease processes. Potential side effects of medications prescribed to our client included: drowsiness, low energy, depression, kidney strain, urinary wastage of essential minerals such as magnesium (Mg) and potassium (K), increased blood cholesterol levels, muscle weakness and many more.

Often, coronary heart disease patients have severe enough disease to necessitate invasive procedures and most all need medications. The treatment approaches that get to the root causes of atheroscerotic heart disease are treatments that reverse atherosclerosis on a systemic (whole-body) level. These systemic treatments include smoking cessation, a whole food plant-based (vegan) diet without refined foods (such as added sugar, refined carbohydrates & oil), exercise, decreasing serum cholesterol levels (via diet, herbs or medication), intermittent fasting, control of hypertension & diabetes, and chelation therapy.

Our patient was treated with a whole food, vegan diet: he consumed no animal products and no refined foods. This particular diet has repeatedly been proven to prevent and reverse atherosclerosis, coronary arterial heart disease and hypertension. He was given essential vitamins, minerals and trace elements to keep his cellular operations at top notch levels and replenish magnesium levels in his body. Although his new diet was high in antioxidant bioflavonoids, extra antioxidants like vitamin C, vitamin E, glutathione, carotenoids and selenium were given to maximize his detoxification pathways, thereby facilitating the discharge of toxic elements from his cells.

Our patient received 30 plus intravenous (IV) Mg-EDTA (magnesium ethylene-diamine-tetraacetic acid) chelation therapy sessions. Recent clinical studies have verified positive clinical effects (efficacy) of Mg-EDTA chelation therapy in reversing atherosclerotic coronary arterial heart disease. Myself and many other physicians have observed, first hand, IV Mg-EDTA chelation therapy helping to reverse hypertension, coronary heart disease, carotid artery heart disease (clogged arteries in the neck supplying the brain), peripheral artery disease (clogged arteries supplying the legs and feet), E.D. (clogged arteries supplying the genitals), diabetic foot ulcers with gangrene, and even severe eczema.

IV Mg-EDTA chelation therapy works by ridding the body of toxic elements such as lead and cadmium. Lead and cadmium initiate and promote the progression of arterial atherosclerosis by inflaming the inner lining of arteries (called the endothelium). Ridding the body of cadmium and lead as well as arsenic, aluminum and other toxic elements by chelation therapy increases the efficiency of enzymes throughout the body.

Results:
- Our patient was gradually weaned completely off all seven(7) of his medications and the wheelchair within three or four months.
- He remained medication free, with no signs or symptoms of either heart disease or hypertension and was observed working as a volunteer at a local health food cooperative store (Sevananda in Atlanta, GA) at the age of 98 years old!

5. HEALTHY EATING:
PLANT-BASED WHOLE FOODS

The key to healthy eating is to consume whole, unprocessed foods. Use organic foods whenever possible. Consume plenty of vegetables and fresh fruits in volumes near equal to the consumption volume of our primary energy sources of whole food starches: legumes, yams, sweet & other potatoes, and whole grains. The paradigm for healthy eating has shifted away from processed and refined "foods" (that have been stripped of fiber, protein, beneficial fats, vitamins, and minerals) to REAL FOOD: Unprocessed, Whole Foods that are alive, such as. . . .

LEAFY GREEN VEGETABLES

Kale (black, purple, red, and green), Collard Greens, Arugula, Spinach, Beet Greens, Mustard Greens, Salad Greens, Swiss Chard, Turnip Greens, Radicchio, Parsley, Cilantro, Lettuce: Green Leaf, Red Leaf, Bibb, Endive, Mixed Baby Lettuce with Herbs, Romaine.

CRUCIFEROUS VEGETABLES

Arugula, Bok Choy, Broccoli, Brussels Sprouts, Cabbage, Cauliflower, Collards, Radishes, Watercress, Kohlrabi.

HERBS - LIVE AND WHOLE

Basil, Burdock, Fennel, Thyme, Rosemary, Chives, Oregano, Endive, Savory, Stevia Leaf, Sage.

PEPPER FRUITS

Bell Pepper, Jalapeno Pepper, Chili Pepper, Cayenne Pepper, Banana Pepper.

SQUASH

Zucchini, Yellow, Spaghetti, Acorn, Butternut.

WILD HERBS, GREENS, AND EDIBLE FLOWERS

Burdock, Curly Dock, Plantain, Red Clover, Marigolds, Dandelions, Artichokes, Asparagus, Honeysuckle, Kudzu, Violas, Sage, Arugula.

STARCHY & OTHER VEGETABLES

Carrots, Okra, Snap Peas, String beans. Garlic, Onions, Shallot, Mushrooms (Button, Oyster, Portobello and Shiitake), Yams, Celery, Sweet Potatoes, Yellow and White Potatoes, Winter Squashes.

FATTY FRUITS

Avocado, Olives, Chocolate (pure), Coconut.

MELONS (Non Sweet and Sweet)

Bitter Melon, Cucumber, Watermelon, Cantaloupe, Yellow, Honeydew, and more.

BERRY FRUITS

Acai, Barberries, Blackberries, Cherries, Raspberries, Strawberries, Blueberries, Goji berries, Muscadines, Gooseberries, Grapes.

OTHER FRUITS

Apples, Grapefruit, Kiwifruit, Lemons, Limes, Plums, Passion Fruit, Pomegranate, Lychees, Tomatoes, Oranges, Tangerines, Tangelos, Apricot, and many more.

LEGUMES (Beans, Lentils and Peas)

Black Beans, Chickpeas (Garbanzo Beans), English peas, Lentils (green, red, French), Kidney Beans, Edamame, Sprouted Organic Tofu, Organic Tempeh, Navy Beans, Red Beans, Adzuki Beans.

WHOLE GRAINS

Barley, Buckwheat, Millet, Oats, Quinoa, Teff, Wild rice, Brown Rice, Spelt, Whole Grain Products: Sprouted Ezekiel Bread and Whole Grain Pasta.

SPROUTS

Sunflower, Mung Bean, Clover, Broccoli, Organic SoyBeans, Wheat Berries.

SEA VEGETABLES

Irish Moss, Nori, Wakame, Arame, Dulse, Algae-Oil Omega 3 Supplements.

NUTS AND SEEDS

Almonds, Brazil Nuts, Cashews, Chia Seeds, **Flax Seeds**, **Hemp Seeds**, Macadamia Nuts, **Pecans, Pistachios, Pumpkin Seeds**, Sesame Seeds (including Raw Tahini), Sunflower Seeds, **Walnuts.**

HERBS AND SPICES

Allspice, Barberries, Bay Leaves, Cardamon, Chili, Cinnamon, Coriander, Cumin, Curry, Dill, Fenugreek, Ginger, Horseradish, Marjoram, Mustard Powder, Nutmeg, Oregano, Pepper, Peppermint, Rosemary, Saffron, Sage, Thyme, Turmeric, Vanilla, and many more.

BEVERAGES

Purified or Spring Water, Green Tea, Herbal tea, lemonade made with non-sugar sweetener (such as the Nasty Lemonade brand), Coffee, Raw Coconut Water.

UNREFINED FOODS PREVENT CHRONIC DISEASES

Complex carbohydrates, such as Barley, Oats, Yams, and Lentils are our primary energy and protein sources. They raise the blood sugar levels more slowly than refined carbohydrates such as white rice, sugar, honey, and frosted corn flakes and are therefore preventive in the development of obesity, type 2 diabetes, and other metabolic diseases. Many populations, worldwide, traditionally consume diets containing large amounts of unrefined, complex carbohydrates with essentially a zero prevalence of obesity and type 2 diabetes.[64] Seventy to ninety-five percent (70% - 95%) of their energy intake may come from whole, unprocessed carbohydrate foods such as sweet potatoes, cassava, yams, coconut, and other whole fruits.[65] In addition, when eating to reverse type 2 diabetes, obesity, hypertension, and other chronic Western diseases, be sure to consume lots of green leafy and cruciferous vegetables, high antioxidant containing foods: berries, greens, tomatoes, sweet potatoes, whole pomegranates (including chewing and consuming the seeds), and smaller amounts of healthy fats: raw nuts, seeds, and avocados.

CONCLUSION

Give yourself at least one month to stick with the consumption of whole plant-based foods. Your lab values and blood pressure will improve. You will feel great and your tastes will begin changing. You will find that eating truly healthy foods tastes better the longer you stick with it. Use the information in the Resources Section to inform, inspire, and empower you to make healthy changes for yourself and your family. It is all up to you!

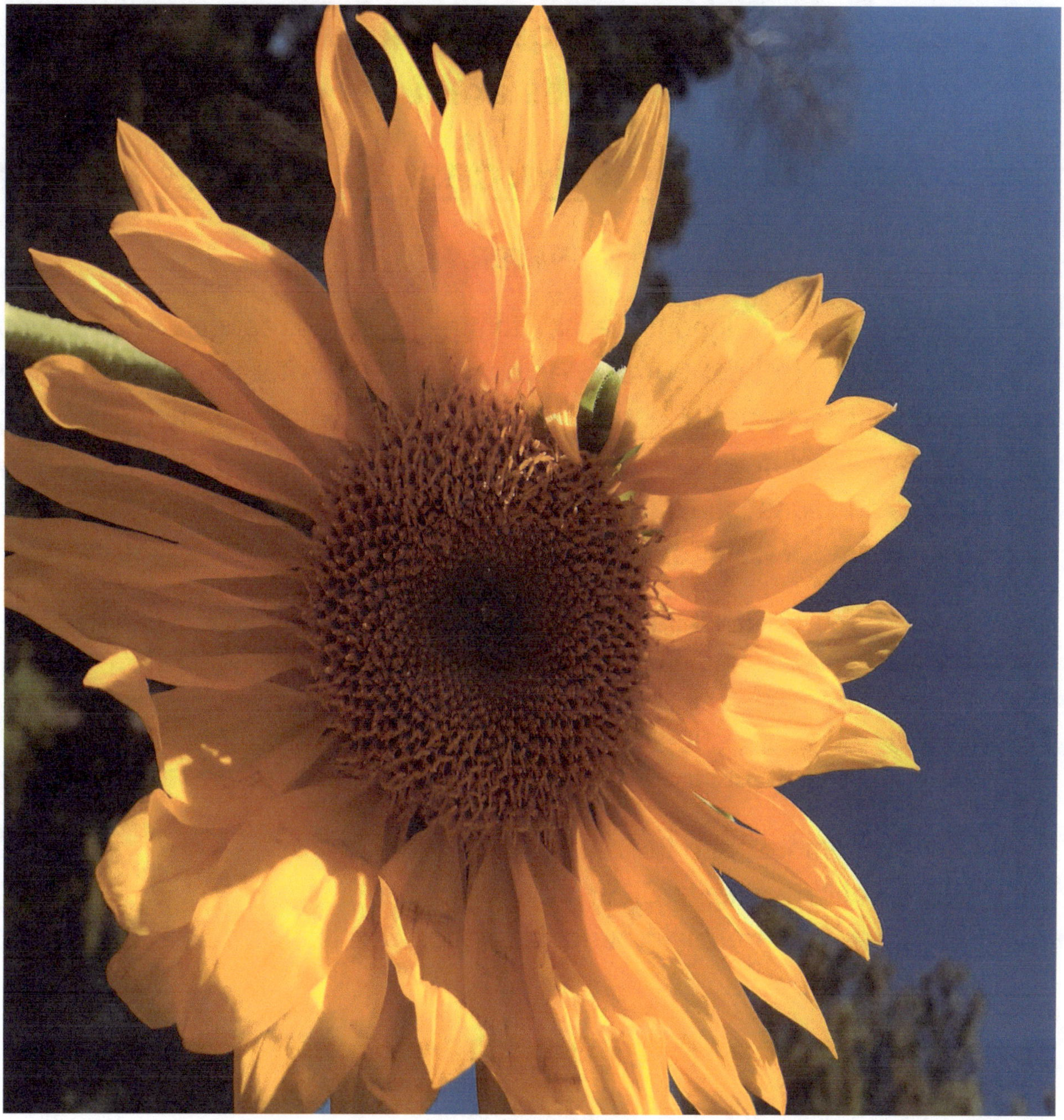

RECIPES

- Use organic foods whenever possible -
- May use more or less amounts of ingredients -

Smoothies, Juices, & Drinks

WATER

Drink water throughout the day to stay hydrated; especially when you first wake up, and about 20 minutes before meals. After meals, allow your food to digest for 1 to 1 ½ hours before drinking large amounts of water. Drinking large volumes of water and other liquids just after eating may contribute to indigestion, gastro-esophageal reflux and heartburn. Sipping smaller amounts of water during meals is usually fine.

Use purified (Distillation-Filtration) water, soft (non-mineralized) spring water, or well water (verified pure).

It's suggested to <u>mostly</u> drink water plain. You may add <u>small amounts</u> of the following ingredients to water:

- Limes, Lemons, and their juices,
- Raw, unfiltered Apple Cider Vinegar,
- Chia seeds or freshly ground flax seeds: 1-2 tsp, in one(1) cup or so of water.

HERBAL TEA

Green tea - Antioxidant, suppresses appetite.

Chai tea - Helps lower blood sugar levels, suppresses craving for sweets.

Peppermint tea - Helps alleviate GI discomfort such as gas and bloating, suppresses appetite.

SUPER GREEN JUICE (not a whole food)

INGREDIENTS:

5-7 - Leaves of Kale (organic Lacinato, Red leaf, or Green leaf)

4-5 - Celery stalks

1 - handful of Cilantro or Parsley

1 - Cucumber, sliced

1 - Green Apple, chopped into quarters

1 - lemon, peeled

1 - inch piece of Ginger

DIRECTIONS:

Wash all the ingredients. Run the ingredients through a juicer.

PINEAPPLE GREEN CLEANSE JUICE (not a whole food)

INGREDIENTS:

3 - Chunks of Pineapple

5 - Cups Spinach, Kale, and/or Collards

1 - Orange, skinned & quartered

1 - Cucumber, sliced

1 ½ inch - piece of Ginger

1 - Lime skinned

1-2 - Dashes of Cayenne

1 - Cup of Ice

DIRECTIONS:

Wash all the ingredients. Run the ingredients (except ice) through a juicer.

Blend the juice with Ice in a blender.

RAINBOW HEALTH JUICE (not a whole food)

INGREDIENTS:

1- Beet Root

2 - Apples

4-5 - Carrots, medium size

1 - Orange, skinned

1 ½ inch - piece of Ginger

1 ½ inch - piece of Turmeric root

DIRECTIONS:

Wash all the ingredients. Run the ingredients through a juicer. May dilute with water or ice.

NAIROBI WHOLE FOODS SMOOTHIE

INGREDIENTS:

2 Cups - Water

1 - Mango, skinned and quartered

1 - Orange, skinned and quartered

1½ Cups - of Frozen Mixed Berries

1 - Lime, skinned and halved

2-3 Tbsp - Whole Hemp Seeds

1 Tbsp - Whole Flax Seeds

1 ½ inches - piece of Ginger

1 ½ - Cups of Ice

DIRECTIONS:

Blend in a high speed blender. Serves 3 - 4.

KIWI COCONUT DELIGHT

INGREDIENTS:

2 to 3 - Kiwis, skinned and halved

1 - Granny Smith Apple, sliced into quarter pieces.

½ - Honeycrisp Apple

¼ - Coconut meat, from a mature (brown) coconut.

Choose one with lots of liquid inside. To break open, place the whole brown coconut in a plastic bag & throw it up and allow it to hit the concrete to break open. Scrape out the coconut meat. May refrigerate or freeze (in an airtight container)

½-1 Fresh Ginger

4 - grams of vitamin C powder

Green Stevia to taste - up to 1 teaspoon , vanilla Stevia Extract

DIRECTIONS:

1. Blend and drink as desired. May refrigerate leftovers in glass containers

SUPER GREEN SMOOTHIE

For a quick nutritious meal, try this wholesome smoothie:

INGREDIENTS: (for 2 servings; cut amounts in half for 1 serving).

3 Cups - Choice/Combination of <u>Unsweetened:</u> Pea Protein, Almond, or Oat Milk / Green Tea / Water / Coconut Water.

4 to 5 Cups - Greens - Choice of: Kale, Spinach, Collards, Arugula, or a combination of any Dark Greens.

2 Cups - Fresh or Frozen Berries.

¼ or ⅓ - Avocado or Banana.

¼ Cup of any combination of <u>whole</u> Flax, Chia, and Hemp seeds. These seeds are loaded with essential fatty acids which reduce inflammation.

1 to 2 scoops - Vegan Protein Powder such as Organic Pea, Hemp, and Sprouted brown Rice or Metabolic Detox Complete*.

2 to 3 tsp - **THRIVE Adaptogen Powder*** or **Moringa Powder*** (Nutrient Dense Green Superfoods)

½ Cup - Ice Cubes.

Other Optional Ingredients:

1 tsp. Vegan DHA Oil - Omega 3 Essential Fatty Acid from SeaWeed Greens. (UDO's brand or another).

½ to 1 - Raw Jalapeno Peppers.

½ to 1 Tbsp - Raw Cacao seeds, powder, or nibs (chocolate) &/or cinnamon

1 small bunch - Fresh Mint Leaves.

* - May order from www.ACPM.net - see Resources and Information Section.

DIRECTIONS:

1. Blend until smooth.
2. Split in half and place in two(2) separate glass containers and refrigerate.
3. Be well hydrated (with water) before consuming.
4. Drink the smoothie slowly - mix with your saliva; wait about one(1) hour before consuming significant amounts of other food.
5. May keep refrigerated for up to six(6) to eight(8) hours.

COMMENTS:

- You may build up to five(5) cups of dark greens.
- This Super Green Smoothie is full of antioxidants, essential fatty acids, vitamins, minerals, and plant-based protein.

Remember to "chew" your smoothies, and mix with saliva before swallowing.

It should take the same amount of time to consume a smoothie as it would to thoroughly chew the solid constituents of the smoothie.

GREEN BERRY BLAST SHAKE

INGREDIENTS:

1 Cup - Purified or Spring Water				Juice of 1/2 Lime

1 Scoop - Metabolic Detox Complete or other vegan protein powder

2 Cups - Baby Spinach or other Dark greens			1/2 Cup - Walnuts

¾ Cups - Frozen Strawberries, Blueberries		1/2 tsp - Raw Green Stevia

1 Cup - Plain, Raw Coconut Yogurt				1/2 Cup - Ice Cubes

DIRECTIONS:

Blend in a high powered blender and slowly drink, mixing each mouthful with saliva.

IRISH MOSS VANILLA SHAKE

INGREDIENTS:

½ cup - Irish Moss (Seaweed) - Soak overnight and thoroughly rinse

1 - Young Coconut or 1 cup of raw unsweetened coconut water

½ cup - Raw Almonds (soaked overnight or unsoaked)

1 - Vanilla Bean (dried) and/or 1 heaping tsp of cacao powder (optional).

1 - Scoop Metabolic Detox Complete*, or other Plant-based Protein Powder

¼ to ½ tsp. Green Stevia (optional).   2 Cups - Purified Water

DIRECTIONS:

1. Open the Coconut and place the liquid or raw coconut water in a large blender(such as a Vitamix) and add the almonds. Add 2 cups of water.
2. Place 1/2 of all of the soft non=liquid contents of the Coconut into the blender.
3. Add the Vanilla Bean and Irish Moss.
4. Add the Stevia (optional).
5. Blend until all contents are a smoothie consistency.
6. Keep unused portions refrigerated 1 to 2 days (shake before use).

SWEET POTATO SMOOTHIE

INGREDIENTS:

1 - Medium-sized Sweet Potato, washed and chopped

1-2 - Medjool Dates, pitted   1 tsp - Cinnamon powder

1-1 ½ - Cups of Water   ¼ Cup non dairy unsweetened milk

⅓ Cup - of Raw Cashews

¼ tsp - Nutmeg powder

3 drops - Vanilla extract

1 tsp - Lemon juice

1 pinch salt

DIRECTIONS:

Blend ingredients in a high powered blender until smooth. May refrigerate for ½ - 1 hour to chill.

Dressings, Sauces & Dips

Photo by Simply Zee Imagery

TAHINI LEMON DRESSING

INGREDIENTS:

4 Tbsp - Sesame Seeds   2 Tbsp - Almonds (soaked for 30 minutes)

3 Garlic Cloves   2 tsp - Mustard Powder

1 Tbsp - Apple Cider Vinegar   1 Tbsp - White Miso

3 Tbsp - Lemon Juice   1 - Cup of Water

1 Tbsp - Nutritional Yeast Flakes (optional)

DIRECTIONS:

Blend in a High Speed Blender. Serve over salad or vegetables.

RASPBERRY SUPREME DRESSING

INGREDIENTS:

1 ½ to 2 Cups - Fresh or frozen Raspberries 1 - Apple, cored & quartered

2 - Medjool Dates, pitted 1 - Garlic clove, skinned

1 tsp - Dijon Mustard 1 Cup - Water

2 Tbsp - apple Cider Vinegar 2 tsp - Fresh Lime Juice

DIRECTIONS:

Blend in a High Speed Blender. Serve over salads.

CREAMY ITALIAN DRESSING

INGREDIENTS:

1 Cup - raw Cashews, almonds, sunflower seeds, or cooked white beans(for a lower fat version). Soak nuts for at least 30 minutes.

1 ½ Cups - Water 3 Tbsp - Balsamic Vinegar

1 tsp - Dried Oregano ½ - ¾ - tsp Sea Salt ½ tsp - Black Pepper

DIRECTIONS:

Blend all ingredients until creamy.   Add additional salt/pepper to taste.

CASHEW "RANCH" DRESSING

INGREDIENTS:

1 Cup - White beans, precooked

1 Cup - Spring/Purified Water

½ Cups - raw Cashews (soaked 30 minutes)

1 Tbsp - Apple Cider Vinegar

1 Tbsp - Lemon Juice

1 ½ tsp - Onion Powder

2-3 Cloves - Garlic or ½ tsp Garlic Powder

1 tsp - Dried Dill Herb

1 tsp - Sea Salt

½ tsp - Dried Basil

¼ tsp - Black Pepper

For a hotter-spicier dressing, add a little Chipotle(smoked dried Jalapenos) seasoning or raw Jalapeno to taste.

DIRECTIONS;

Blend all ingredients until smooth and creamy, but before it gets hot.

Add more water to thin as needed.

HUMMUS-ORANGE DRESSING

INGREDIENTS:

½ Cup - plain, oil-free Hummus

2 - Tbsp Balsamic Vinegar

2 peeled, de-seeded organic Oranges

2 tsp - Dijon Mustard

½ Cup Spring/Purified Water

1 tsp - fresh grated Ginger

1-2 - cloves of Garlic

Sea Salt to taste

Ground Pepper to taste

DIRECTIONS:

Blend all ingredients together. Taste, and add salt and pepper to taste.

CASHEW CREAM SAUCE

INGREDIENTS:

2 Cups - Raw, Unsalted Cashews in water overnight and chilled

6 Tbsp - Lemon Juice ¾ Cup - Cold, purified or spring water

½ - 1 tsp - Fine Sea Salt ½ tsp - Nutritional Yeast (optional)

DIRECTIONS:

1. Drain cashews and place in a blender with the Lemon Juice, Nutritional yeast, water, and Sea Salt.
2. Puree until smooth, at least three(3) minutes, adding more water, 1 Tbsp at a time until sauce is thick and smooth.
3. Taste and carefully season with more Salt or Lemon Juice; the sauce should be tangy, but not sour.
4. Chill for 30 minutes or more before serving.

VEGAN CAESAR DRESSING

INGREDIENTS:

1 Cup - Raw cashews, soaked for 1-2 in advance; then drained. May use white cooked beans(for a lower fat alternative).

1 Cup - unsweetened plant-based milk: Pea, Almond, Soy, or other

2 Tbsp - Nutritional Yeast (optional) 1 Tbsp - Chia Seeds

2 - Cloves of Garlic, chopped ½ tsp - Salt or 1 tsp - Tamari

4 Tbsp - Lemon Juice, freshly squeezed 1-2 - Medjool Dates, pitted

Water or extra milk for thinning, as needed 1 - tsp Kelp granules

DIRECTIONS:

1. Combine the cashews, 1 tbsp of nutritional yeast (if being used), the chia seeds, salt (or Tamari), garlic, pepper, milk, lemon juice, adn dates in a blender, and puree until smooth. May add more nutritional yeast and other condiments as desired.
2. Serve mixed into romain, other lettuce, and other vegetables as desired.
3. May keep in the refrigerator for up to 4 days. Stir in a few tsp of plant-based milk to thin the dressing as desired.

APPLE VINAIGRETTE DRESSING

INGREDIENTS:

1 - large Apple or 2 small Apples, cored and diced   1 Tbsp - mild Miso

1 tsp - ground Cumin   ½ tsp - ground Cinnamon

¼ Cup - Apple Cider Vinegar   2 - Tbsp Balsamic Vinegar

2-3 tsp - Dijon Mustard   2 - Dates, pitted

½ - rounded tsp sea salt   Ground Black Pepper to taste

DIRECTIONS:

1. Place the apples, miso, cumin, cinnamon, apple cider, balsamic vinegar, mustard, dates, salts, and pepper in a high powered blender, and blend until very smooth.
2. Taste and adjust the seasoning. If you desire a thinner dressing, add a couple teaspoons of water and blend again.

CLASSIC DIJON DRESSING

INGREDIENTS:

¼ Cup - Dijon Mustard

¼ Cup - Apple Cider Vinegar

¼ Cup - Water

Juice of 2 Small Lemons or 1 Large Lemon

2 - Dates, pitted

½ tsp - Sea salt

¼ tsp - Black Pepper

½ tsp - ground Thyme

½ tsp - ground Dill

DIRECTIONS:

1. Place the ingredients in a high powered blender, and blend until very smooth.
2. May double or triple the quantities as desired
3. This dressing will keep in the refrigerator for a week.

QUINNIES RAW CHUNKY MARINARA SAUCE

INGREDIENTS:
2 Cups - Fresh Basil, removed from stem
2 Bell Peppers, Red and Yellow
½ Cup - Fresh Oregano, removed from stem
2 Pints - Cherry Tomatoes
3 - carrots, cut in ½ inch chunks
3 Cloves - Garlic
2 tsp - Lemon juice
1 Cup - Chopped Tomatoes
1 Cup - Sun dried Tomatoes, soaked* for 2 hours and drained
4 Medjool Dates, pitted and soaked* for 1 hour and drained
1 tbsp - Miso or 1 tsp sea salt (optional)

INSTRUCTIONS:
1. Place all ingredients in the food processor or blender, except carrots and chopped Tomatoes, and blend well.
2. Add Carrots, then use pulse setting. Carrots should not be completely blended, but in little pieces.
3. Stir in chopped tomatoes to add texture to the blended sauce.

SERVING IDEAS:
1. Serve over Zucchini Spiral Pasta or vegetable(s) of choice
2. Use as a marinade for vegetables, as a salad dressing, or serve over cooked pasta.
3. Make a soup by adding additional warm liquid to desired consistency.
4. Shelf life: 1 week, refrigerated. Can freeze for 1 month.

*Retain soaking water to use in other recipes or use for marinara sauce if a more liquidy consistency of soup is desired. **Quinnieskitchen.com**

SALSA

INGREDIENTS:

2 - Large Fresh Tomatoes, chopped

1 - small to medium red or yellow onion, diced

3 Tbsp - Fresh Lime Juice

2 Tbsp - Fresh Cilantro, chopped

½ - Jalapeno Pepper, pitted and minced

INSTRUCTIONS:

1. Stir ingredients together in a large bowel.
2. Cover and chill.

HUMMUS

INGREDIENTS: (may cut ingredient amounts in half)

1 Cup - Freshly Ground Sesame Seeds

2 to 3 Cups - mashed Garbanzo bean sprouts, or cooked Garbanzo beans

4-6 Cloves - of Garlic, crushed

5-6 - Olives, pitted

2-4 Tbsp - Lemon Juice

2-4 Tbsp - Chopped Parsley   Water- as needed

INSTRUCTIONS:

Mix or blend wet, and then dry ingredients. Consistency should be thick. Mix in the parsley last.

GUACAMOLE

INGREDIENTS:

2 or 3 - Mashed Avocados.

1 - Diced Tomato

½ - Red or Yellow Onion, diced.

2 - Lemons, juiced

¼ Cup - of Finely Diced Hot Peppers or ¼ - tsp of Cayenne Pepper Powder

1-2 Cloves - Garlic, crushed.

2 Tbsp - Cilantro, chopped

Dash of Salt

INSTRUCTIONS:

Mix well and serve.

RAW VEGETABLES

Serve with Dressings, Sauces, and Dips

Broccoli florets

Cauliflower florets

Cherry tomatoes, halved

Bell peppers, sliced

Cucumber slices

Carrot sticks

Celery sticks

Radish roses

Mushrooms, halved

Zucchini slices

Photo by Simply Zee Imagery

Majestic Salads, Vegetables & Soups

Photo by Simply Zee Imagery

GREENS, PEAS AND WALNUTS SALAD

INGREDIENTS:

2 Cups - Shelled, Fresh Peas (from about 1 lb. of pea pods) - May use thawed Frozen Peas if necessary.

6 Cups - Mixed Spring Greens, other Lettuce Greens, or baby Kale and Spinach Greens. May use Mixtures of Greens.

2 Cups - Three(3) or more types of mixed, Fresh Herb Leaves: Mint, Dill, Parsley, Chervil (French Parsley) and/or Fennel.

1 Bunch - Chives (trimmed and sliced into ½ inch pieces).

Edible Flowers such as : Johnny-Jump-up Violas, Marigolds, Thyme, Sage, Honeysuckle or arugula.

DIRECTIONS:

1. If using Fresh Peas, soak them in purified water for one(1) hour with a pinch of Sea Salt (or may place them in boiling water for 30 seconds to 1 minute - transfer to cool water).
2. Drain Peas and spread out on clean paper towels or a clean kitchen towel and pat dry. If using thawed Frozen Peas, dry them the same way as in an uncooked state.
3. In a large bowl, add the Peas, Greens, Herb Leaves, Edible Flowers, and Chives. Gently toss with your hands.
4. Serve the salad and dress with one of the dressings above.

CURRY CABBAGE & CAULIFLOWER DELIGHT

INGREDIENTS:

½ Head - White Cabbage, chopped

½ Head - Cauliflower, chopped

⅓-½ Head - Broccoli, chopped

2-3 Tbsp - Chickpea Miso or other Miso

2-3 Tbsp - Tahini

½ Cup - Sun-dried Tomatoes, soaked in water for 2-3 hours

2 to 2 ½ cups - Water

DIRECTIONS:

1. Add the chopped cabbage, cauliflower, and broccoli into a large mixing bowl.
2. Mix the other ingredients in a food processor or high-speed blender. Pour over the vegetables, mix and serve.

BALANCED VEGETABLE SALAD WITH WALNUTS, HEMP SEEDS AND AVOCADO

INGREDIENTS:

4 Cups - Dark Green Lettuce of choice: green or Red Leaf, Romaine, Bibb, Escarole, sliced or torn in strips

2 Cups - Broccoli and/or Cauliflower, chopped in small pieces

2 Cups - Sunflower or Mung Bean Sprouts   1 Cup - Sliced red Onions

1 Cup - Cubed Zucchini squash   1 Cup - Tomatoes, sliced

1 Cup - Crushed Walnuts   1 Avocado, diced

DIRECTIONS:

Combine and toss ingredients in a large bowl.

Use one of the non-oil dressings in the **Dressings, Sauces & Dips** recipe section above.

KALE SALAD WITH AVOCADO, WALNUTS, AND TOMATOES

INGREDIENTS:

6 Cups - Kale, cleaned and chopped

1 - Medium to large Tomato, diced (optional)

3 Tbsp - Apple Cider or Balsamic Vinegar

Fresh Sage   Himalayan Salt

1 - Large Avocado diced

1 Cup - Walnuts, crushed

2 Tbsp - White Miso

Black Pepper, ground

DIRECTIONS:

1. In a large mixing bowl, toss the Kale, Walnuts and Tomato and mix together.
2. Add the Avocado, Vinegar, Miso and Sage and mix together using your hands.
3. Season as desired with Sage, Salt and Pepper.

CURRY BROCCOLI & SPINACH IN CASHEW CREAM SAUCE

INGREDIENTS:

1 ½ lbs. - Broccoli, Broccolini (Baby Broccoli), and/or Purple Broccoli

8 oz. - Baby Spinach

¾ Cup - Cashews, Raw, w/o salt, roughly chopped

1 - Medium-sized Lime, quartered

1 Cup - Cilantro Leaves

1 - 1 ½ Tbsp - Madras Curry powder or other seasonings

Cashew Cream Sauce in the **Dressings, Sauces & Dips** recipe section above - Mix in as desired.

Dulse Flakes   Dash of salt

DIRECTIONS:

1. Wash, drain, and rinse Broccoli. Cut Broccoli into three(3) inch lengths and halve thick stems lengthwise. Place in a large mixing bowl.
2. Squeeze 2 lime quarters while drizzling the lime juice over the Broccoli. Season with a couple of pinches of salt and toss.
3. Add the Spinach, half of the chopped Cashews, and three-fourths of both the Cilantro and Curry.
4. With a large serving spoon, spread about 1 cup of the Cashew cream onto a shallow serving platter. Use the back of the spoon to spread into a thick bed for the salad. Pile salad across cream and scatter with the remaining crushed Cashews and Cilantro. Garnish with a small amount of Dulse Flakes.

GREENS WITH BERRIES SALAD

INGREDIENTS:

6 Cups - Mixed Baby Greens, Baby Kale, and /or Baby Spinach

6 Cups - Green Leaf or Romaine Lettuce

1 ½ to 2 Cups - Fresh Raspberries, Blueberries, and or chopped Strawberries.

1 ½ Cups - Cherry Tomatoes, halved

½ - Medium Red Onion, diced.   ½ Cup - raw walnuts, crushed

DIRECTIONS:

In a large mixing bowl, toss the Salad ingredients, except the walnuts, and mix together. Sprinkle the walnuts over the salad.

Serve with the Raspberry Supreme Dressing (see recipe above), or dressing of choice.

MIGHTY GREEN SALAD

INGREDIENTS:

4 Cups - Mixed Lettuce (Romaine, Bibb, Green/Red Leaf), chopped

1 Cup - Cabbage, Shredded

1 - Medium Zucchini, diced

2 - Bell Peppers, Red/Orange/yellow, diced

2 - Kohlrabi, diced

1 - Avocado, peeled and diced

1 Cup - Swiss Chard, diced

1 Cup - Kale, chopped.

2 Cups - Spinach, chopped

½ Cup - String Beans, diced

¼ Cup - Chives, diced

½ Cup - Fresh Peas

1 Cup - Fresh Mung beans, or other Sprouts

DIRECTIONS:

1. Combine all the ingredients in a large bowl.
2. Serve with your favorite dressing.

RAW CARROT SALAD

INGREDIENTS:

2 Pounds carrots, peeled and grated.

1 - onion, diced fine

1 tsp - Lemon Juice, or Apple Cider Vinegar.

2 - Stalks Celery, diced.

¼ tsp - sea salt

¼ Cup - Tahini

¼ tsp - dill weed

4 Tbsp - Lightly-Salted Tamari.

¼ tsp - Garlic Powder

DIRECTIONS:

1. Combine all the ingredients in a large bowl until creamy and crunchy.
2. Chill and serve.

SPINACH MUSHROOM SALAD

INGREDIENTS:

1 Pound - Fresh Spinach, chopped

1 - Head Green Lettuce, shredded

2 - Bell Peppers, Red/Orange/yellow, diced

5 - Tomatoes, cut into chunks

½ Pound - Fresh Mushrooms, sliced

¼ - Head Cabbage, shredded

2 - Garlic Cloves, finely diced

DIRECTIONS:

1. Add all the ingredients into a large bowl - except the Tomatoes - and toss. If time, chill all ingredients for 1 hour.
2. Serve with your favorite dressing. Top with tomatoes.

CREAMY TANGY COLESLAW

INGREDIENTS:

3 Cups - Chopped Green Cabbage

1 ¾ Cups - Carrots, grated

1 ½ Cups - Diced cored Apple; unpeeled or peeled

1 Cup - Chopped Red Cabbage

½ Cup - Finely chopped Red Cabbage

½ Cup - Finely chopped Red Onion

Dressing Ingredients:

½ Cup - Water

2 Ounces - Raw unsalted Cashews or ¾ cups of cooked white bean for a lower fat version

2 Tbsp - Mustard, Dijon or Stone Ground

1 Tbsp - Apple Cider Vinegar; may substitute another vinegar

1-2 - Medium Cloves of Garlic, minced.

DIRECTIONS:

1. Place all of the dressing ingredients (water, cashews, mustard, vinegar, and garlic) into a blender - set aside for 15 to 20 minutes to soften the cashews.
2. Place all of the salad ingredients (green and red cabbage, carrots, apple, raisins, and onion) into a large bowel.
3. Blend the dressing ingredients until smooth, and pour the dressing over the salad and mix well.
4. May add ¼ cup of thinly sliced celery, or ½ cup of chopped bell pepper, cauliflower, or broccoli for variation.

GAZPACHO SOUP

INGREDIENTS:

4 Cups - of Tomatoes, chopped   4 - Garlic Cloves

½ Cup - Yellow Onion, chopped.   1 - Cucumber, skinned & chopped

1 - Zucchini or Yellow Squash   ½ Cup - of Chopped Celery

½ Cup - Red, Orange, or Yellow Bell Pepper   ½ Cup - of White Cabbage

Basil, Thyme, Tamari, and Cayenne to taste.

DIRECTIONS:

1. Blend ingredients.
2. Add more chopped skinned cucumber and/or zucchini/yellow squash.
3. Decorate with chopped parsley.

CREAM OF BROCCOLI SOUP

INGREDIENTS:

2 Cups - chopped Broccoli - You can also substitute broccoli with other vegetables such as carrots, celery, kale, or spinach.

1 - Avocado, pitted and skinned.			1 Tbsp - Tahini

2 Cups - Sprouts: Mung beans, Alfalfa, Lentils, Broccoli, Garbanzo beans, etc.

1 tsp - Kelp powder			¼ tsp - Cayenne pepper (optional)

DIRECTIONS:

1. Blend until smooth. Add the avocado last.
2. You can decorate with slices of mushrooms, chopped cilantro or parsley.

CREAM OF SPINACH SOUP

INGREDIENTS:

1 lb - Spinach (about 15 cups)	1 Tbsp - Tahini
2 Cups - of Water	¼ Cup - Onion
¼ Cup - of Celery	1 tsp - dried parsley flakes
1-2 - Cloves of Garlic	½ tsp - dried Oregano
½ tsp - of Black Pepper	¼ tsp - Salt

DIRECTIONS:

Blend until smooth.

TOMATO SOUP

INGREDIENTS:

4 - Tomatoes, chopped

¼ Cup- of chopped Chives

1 Tbsp - Tahini

½ Cup - Carrots, diced

2 - Garlic Cloves

½ - Red or Yellow Onion, chopped

2 tsp - chopped fresh Thyme or ½ tsp. dried

1 Tbsp - Fresh Oregano or basil, chopped

2 - more Tomatoes, **diced** (Reserve - do not blend)

½ Cup - Cashews

1 - Medjool Date, pitted

1 Cup - Water

½ Cup - Celery, diced

½ - Lemon or lime, juiced

½ tsp - Salt. (optional)

DIRECTIONS:

1. Blend all ingredients (except the 2 diced tomatoes) until smooth.
2. Add the reserved diced tomatoes and gently stir.

Main Dishes: Wholesome & Nutritious

MEXICAN BREAKFAST SPECIAL

INGREDIENTS:

2 Cups - Pinto beans, mashed

8-10 Soft whole-grain corn tortillas

1 tub, about 14 ozs - Organic/Non-GMO Firm Tofu, drained and crushed

½ Cup - Vegetable broth

½ Cup - Yellow onions, chopped

½ Cup - Scallions, chopped

1 tsp - Chile powder   Salsa - Fresh (see recipe above) or buy

1 tsp Soy sauce (optional)   Freshly ground pepper

½ tsp - Turmeric powder   Sea salt (optional)

DIRECTIONS:

1. Drain the tofu well, and mash with your hands or large fork and place in a bowl.
2. Gently heat the pinto beans in a saucepan.
3. Place the vegetable broth in a large non-stick pan, add the onions & scallions, and slowly cook. Stir frequently for a few minutes until softened. Add the tofu and seasonings to taste. Continue to cook while mixing well & stirring frequently for a few more minutes..
4. Heat tortillas by baking on low heat(200-250) for about 10 minutes.
5. To assemble: Place one tortilla on a plate. Spread the beans on the tortilla. Top with the tofu mixture. Top with salsa as desired.

LENTIL-WALNUT NO-MEAT

INGREDIENTS:

1 ½ Cups - dry Brown Lentils, 2 Cups Canned Lentils, or 3 - Cups Sprouted Lentils

2 Cups - Walnuts, raw

1 ½ Tbsp - Oregano, cut and sifted or ½ Cup of fresh Oregano

1 ½ Tbsp - Ground Cumin   1 Tbsp - Chili Powder

2 Tbsp - Nutritional yeast   1 tsp - Tamari or Coconut Aminos

2 Tbsp - Water or more as needed

DIRECTIONS:

1. Place the walnuts in a food processor, pulsing several times - chipping them up.
2. Add 2-4 Tbsp water as needed, facilitating even mixing.
3. For cooked dry lentils: preferably soak in water for 4 - 12 hours prior to preparation. Drain soaked lentils and add enough water to double the volume. Bring to a boil and cook for ½ hour or until tender.
4. Add the seasonings and mix thoroughly.
5. Use as a non-meat protein source in lunches & dinner, as a sandwich spread, in burritos, tacos, may form into "burgers", etc.

VEGETARIAN TOFU AND STEAMED VEGETABLES

INGREDIENTS:

1 Tub - Organic (Non-GMO) Sprouted firm TOFU, diced

2 Cups - organic Kale, chopped

2 Cups - organic Broccoli, chopped

4 - Medium Carrots, chopped into bite-sized pieces

1 - Medium Red Onion, diced

2 - Garlic Cloves, finely diced

1 inch piece - Ginger, finely diced

2 tsp - Himalayan Salt

1 - 2 tsp - Curry powder

Other spices as desired

1/2 Cup - purified water

DIRECTIONS:

1. Stir-Fry 1/2 the Onion, 1 Clove of Garlic and 1/2 the Ginger and 1 tsp. Salt in water and add TOFU.
2. Steam the Kale, Broccoli, carrots, 1/2 the Onion, Clove of Garlic and 1/2 the Ginger in with the TOFU. Add more vegetable broth or water as needed. Add salt to taste.

ZUCCHINI PASTA WITH AVOCADO, PUMPKIN SEED PESTO AND MARINARA SAUCE

INGREDIENTS:

2 - Zucchini - made into "pasta" using a spiralizer or just slicing with a knife

1 - Avocado, ripened

Pumpkin Seed Pesto - see recipe below

1 jar - Marinara Sauce - low fat, no added sugar. May use the recipe above

1 ½ Cup - Walnuts, crushed

DIRECTIONS:

1. Place the Zucchini pasta on a dinner plate.
2. Add Tomato Sauce over the zucchini and the Pesto on the side as desired.
3. Sprinkle on the crushed walnuts as desired.
4. Slice Avocado over Zucchini Pasta as desired.

PUMPKIN SEED PESTO

INGREDIENTS:

2 Cups - Fresh Basil Leaves   4 Cloves - Fresh Garlic

½ Cup - Pumpkin Seeds, soaked and drained

½ - Peeled Lemon   ½ tsp - Lemon Zest

½ inch - Fresh Turmeric Root or ½ tsp Turmeric Powder

½ Cup - Pinto Beans, cooked, not warm   ½ cup - Spring/Purified Water

2 Tbsp - White Miso   Pepper to taste

DIRECTIONS:

Combine all ingredients in a food processor; blend until smooth.

BAKED (whole grain) BROWN RICE

INGREDIENTS: (may bake more or less rice - 2/1 ratio of water/rice)
4 Cups - **Brown Basmati Rice** - May mix with or use other types of whole grain rice such as **Red Rice**, **Black Japonica rice** and/or **dark Brown Wehani rice** for a total of 4 cups of rice. May cook **Bulgur** the same way.
8 Cups - Water

DIRECTIONS:
1. Preheat the oven to 400 degrees.
2. Place 4 Cups of brown Basmati and other whole grain rice into a 2 inch deep baking pan.   Add 8 Cups of Water.
3. Cover with aluminum foil with a small open area for steam to escape.
4. Bake for about 1 hour.
5. Store unused portions in the refrigerator for use within 2 days. May freeze for longer storage in an airtight container.

BEANS & BULGUR SALAD

INGREDIENTS:

4 Cups - Bulgur, cooked and cooled. Cook the brown rice recipe above.

3 Cups - ChickPeas, cooked. May obtain from two 15 oz. cans - no added salt.

1 ½ Cups - Small Red Beans, cooked. May obtain from one 15 oz. can - no added salt.

1 Cup - Thinly sliced Celery.

1 Cup - Chopped fresh Parsley and or Cilantro.

½ Cup - Sweet Onion or Red Onion, fine chopped.

¾ Cup Tomato Juice, low-sodium.   3 Tbsp - Apple cider or Sherry Vinegar.

2 Tbsp - Pure Maple Syrup.   1 tsp - Dry Mustard.

½ tsp - Salt.   ¼ tsp - Cayenne Pepper.

Baby Lettuce or Mixed Baby Greens; Cherry Tomatoes, quartered; Black Pepper - freshly ground.

DIRECTIONS:
1. Place all ingredients (except the lettuce/greens, tomatoes, and freshly ground black pepper) in a large mixing bowl and gently mix together.
2. Arrange the Lettuce/Greens on a large serving platter.
3. Top with quartered Cherry Tomatoes and sprinkle with Black Pepper.

BLACKEYE PEA SOUP

INGREDIENTS:

5 Cups - Blackeye Peas or other dry legume	12 Cups - Water
1 - Medium Sweet Potato, dice.	½ - Yellow Onion, diced
5-6 - Cloves of Garlic, crushed	3 Tbsp - Thyme, cut, and sifted
1 - Curry herb leaves branch, unprocessed	2 Tbsp - Curry powder
1 - Rosemary herb stick, unprocessed	2 Tbsp - Onion powder
2 Tbsp - Sage, cut, and sifted	2 Tbsp - Garlic powder
1 ½ Tbsp - Cajun Seasoning	1 Tbsp - Black Pepper
2 tsp - Smoked Paprika	1 tsp - Cumin powder
2 Tbsp - Extra Virgin Olive Oil - optional	½ Tbsp - Salt - optional

DIRECTIONS:

1. Soak the beans in 12 cups of water for 3 or more (up to 24) hours and rinse - or - slowly boil for 15-20 minutes and scoop up the froth with a large spoon and discard.
2. Replace the water and place it on low heat for a slow boil, stirring often.
3. Add the diced sweet potatoes, while stirring.
4. Add the diced onion and garlic cloves.
5. Add all the other seasonings. Vary seasonings as desired.
6. Stir often and cook until the beans are tender enough to smash against the side of the pot, and a fork can go through the potatoes.
7. Serve with brown rice and a large serving of vegetables and salad.

SPLIT PEA OR OTHER BEAN SOUP

INGREDIENTS:

4 Cups - Split Peas or other dry Legume	12 Cups - Water
1 medium - Japanese Sweet Potato, diced	2 Tbsp - Garlic Powder
1 medium - Orange Sweet Potato, diced	5-6 - Cloves of Garlic, crushed
1 small - White Onion, skinned, and diced.	3 Tbsp - Thyme, cut and sifted
1-2 Tbsp - Sage or Rosemary, cut and sifted	2 Tbsp - Garlic Powder
2 Tbsp - Onion Powder	2 Tbsp - Cajun Seasoning
1 Tbsp - Black Pepper, crushed	½ Tbsp - Salt, optional

DIRECTIONS:

1. Soak the beans in 12 cups of water for 3 or more (up to 24) hours and rinse - or - slowly boil for 15-20 minutes and scoop up the froth with a large spoon and discard.
2. Replace the water and place it on low heat for a slow boil, stirring often.
3. Add the diced sweet potatoes, while stirring.
4. Add the diced onion and garlic cloves.
5. Add all the other seasonings. Vary seasonings as desired.
6. Stir often and cook until the beans are tender enough to smash against the side of the pot, and a fork can go through the potatoes.
7. Serve with brown rice and a large serving of vegetables and salad.

LENTIL & SPINACH SOUP

INGREDIENTS:

4 Cups - Green Lentils, dry

2 Cups - Carrots, sliced

2 Cups - Broccoli, diced

2 Cups - Red Bell Pepper, diced

12 Cups - Water

1 Medium - Red Onion, skinned, and diced

6-8 Cloves - Garlic, crushed

3 Tbsp - Thyme, cut and sifted

2 tsp - Turmeric, ground

2 tsp - Cumin, ground

2 Tbsp - Garlic Powder

2 Tbsp - Onion Powder

2 Tbsp - Cajun Seasoning

1 Tbsp - Black Pepper, crushed

1-2 Tbsp - Sage or Rosemary, cut and sifted

DIRECTIONS:

1. Soak the beans in 12 cups of water for 3 or more(up to 24) hours and rinse - or - slowly boil for 15-20 minutes and scoop up the froth with a large spoon and discard.
2. Replace the water and place it on low heat for a slow boil, stirring often.
3. Add the diced carrots, while stirring.
4. Add the diced onion and garlic cloves.
5. Add the diced broccoli, and red bell pepper, while stirring.
6. Add all the other seasonings. Vary seasonings as desired.
7. Stir often and cook until the beans are tender enough to smash against the side of the pot.
8. Serve with a baked sweet potato or over brown rice with a large serving of vegetable salad.

SPAGHETTI WITH VEGETABLE TOFU MARINARA SAUCE

INGREDIENTS: (may cut amounts in half)

Pasta Choices

- 1-2 packs(16 ounces each) - Whole wheat or other whole grain pasta
- 3-4 cups Spiralized zucchini **-** Use a Spiralizer
  https://www.youtube.com/watch?v=Gg2UpyanG7s
- 2-4 packs(8.8 ounces each) - Organic Buckwheat Capellini - non-gluten with superior protein. Buy organic buckwheat and other whole plant products from Health Food Stores and online:
  www.biggreenorganic.com/products/organic-buckwheat-capellini

Vegetable Tofu Sauce

1 tub, about 14 ozs - Organic/Non-GMO Firm Tofu, drained and crushed

8 - Baby Portobello or White Mushrooms, diced

½ large - Orange, Red, or Yellow Bell Pepper, diced

2 Cups - Broccoli florets, chopped into bite size pieces

6 cloves - Garlic, minced fine   2 medium - Yellow Onion, diced

½ Cup - Carrots, chopped   4 Tbsp - Fresh Parsley, chopped

4 Tbsp - Fresh Basil, chopped   3-4 large Kale leaves, chopped

Quinnie's RAW Marinara Sauce (see Recipe above) - or - 2-3 bottles of commercial Pasta sauce: low fat(1g/serving), low sodium, and zero sugar.

Additionally, you may add Curry powder, Italian seasoning, Smoked Paprika, and a dash of salt to taste.

DIRECTIONS:

Sauce

1. Add ½ cup of water to a large cast iron skillet and preheat. Add herbs and spices. Add the onion, bell pepper, and mushrooms and gently stir.
2. After a few minutes add the broccoli and continue stirring, adding more water as needed.
3. Add the spaghetti sauce while gently stirring.
4. Drain and crumble the tofu. Add the tofu to the mixture and add additional spices as desired. Continue stirring.
5. Cover and keep warm. Serve over the pasta or zucchini.

Cooking: whole grain pastas. Spiralized zucchini is eaten raw.

Use cooking instructions on the package of noodles or;

Fill a large stockpot with water and bring to a boil, add a pinch of salt and desired amount of pasta and return to a rolling boil, cook for 5-8 minutes or until desired texture. Separate the pasta gently with a fork during cooking to prevent clumping. Rinse it with cold water to firm up the texture.

108

OPEN-BURRITO DINNER

INGREDIENTS:

- **Baked Tofu Cubes**

1 or 2 - Tubs of Tofu, organic & non-GMO, cubed   Parchment Paper

Onion Powder, Garlic Powder, Cajun Seasoning, Paprika, and Black Pepper to taste.

- **2 to 4, 15.5 oz cans of Organic Black or Pinto Beans, and/or may use the Lentil-Walnut No-Meat** (See Recipe above)
- **One Diced Tomato or Salsa**

For Salsa, see recipe above under Dressings, Sauces, and Dips. Alternatively, use a bottle of low-sodium commercial Salsa.

- **One Sliced Avocado**
- **Water-Sauteed Vegetables**

1 - Red, Orange, or Yellow Bell Pepper, pitted and sliced

1 - Yellow Onion, sliced   ½ - Pack of mushrooms, sliced

½ tsp - Onion Powder   ½ tsp - Garlic powder

½ tsp - Black Pepper   ½ tsp - Salt

1 - Dash of Tamari Sauce as desired   ½ Cup - Water

- **Baked Whole Grain Rice -** see recipe above.
- **Whole Grain Burritos -** store bought.

DIRECTIONS:

Baked Tofu Cubes

1. Preheat the oven to 400 degrees.
2. Cut the tofu tub(s) into ½ inch cubes and place on parchment paper lining a baking pan.

3. Sprinkle the flavorings over all of the tofu cubes.
4. Place the tofu cubes over the pan and bake for 20 -25 minutes.

Water-Sauteed Vegetables

1. Add water, and heat to near boil.
2. Add vegetables and saute, adding seasonings and slowly stirring. Cook until slightly soft.

Black or pinto beans, or use the Lentil-Walnut No-Meat cold or room temperature.

1. Heat the beans in a pot. Season as you wish.

ASSEMBLE THE OPEN BURRITOS

1. Open the burrito and place it on a dinner plate.
2. Add the desired amount of tofu, beans or lentil-walnut no-meat, sauteed vegetables, whole grain rice, tomatoes or salsa, and avocado slices on the burrito.

Desserts: Delectable & Healthy

CHIA PUDDING

INGREDIENTS:

6 Tbsp - Chia Seeds

2 Cups - Unsweetened Almond, Cashew Milk, or Coconut milk

½ tsp - Vanilla Extract

1 Tbsp - (Whole) Date Sugar, ½ tsp - Monk fruit/Erythritol, or another sweetener of choice (optional)

Blueberries and Strawberries for topping

Walnuts (crushed)

DIRECTIONS:

1. In a mixing bowl, mix together Chia Seeds, Milk, Date Sugar (or another sweetener) and Vanilla. Let it sit for 5 minutes; then, give it another stir to break up any clumps of chia Seeds. Cover and allow to sit in the fridge for 1 to 2 hours.
2. Serve in bowls, topped with Berries and Walnuts.

BERRY NUTTY PARFAIT

INGREDIENTS:

1 Cup - Organic, plain (unsweetened) Coconut Yogurt

1 Tbsp - 100% Cocoa Powder (optional)

1 tsp - Pure Vanilla Extract (optional)

10 Almonds - crushed (preferably soaked overnight and skins removed

6 Walnuts - Crushed

3-4 - Strawberries, diced)

½ Cup - Raspberries

½ Cup - Blackberries

½ Cup - Blueberries

1 Tbsp - Flax Seed, grounds (optional)

1 tsp - Cinnamon, ground

½ Tbsp - Chia Seeds (optional)

DIRECTIONS:

1. Place the Coconut Yogurt in a bowl. And stir in the Cocoa Powder and Vanilla Extract (if using).
2. May chill the above mixture in the freezer for thirty(30) minutes on a hot day.
3. Stir the Nuts and Berries into the Coconut Yogurt.
4. Mix in the Ground Flax seed and Chia Seeds (if using).
5. Sprinkle the Cinnamon over the top.

RAW SWEET POTATO PIE

INGREDIENTS:

Crust

1 Cup - Raw Walnuts, pecans, or walnuts - ideally soaked and dehydrated

1/2 Cup - Rolled Oats - soaked in ¾ cup of water overnight

½ Cup - Dates - pitted and soaked for at least 20 minutes

½ tsp - Vanilla extract or ½ of an organic vanilla bean - scraped

½ tsp - Cinnamon - ground

¼ tsp - salt

Filling

3 Cups - Sweet Potatoes - scrubbed, peeled and diced

6 - Dates - pitted and soaked for at least 20 minutes.

⅓ Cup - Non-dairy Milk(Pea, Almond, Cashew…) - unsweetened

2 tsp - Cinnamon - ground

2 tsp - Lemon juice

1/2 tsp - Vanilla extract or ½ of an organic vanilla bean - scraped

¼ tsp - Nutmeg - ground

DIRECTIONS:

Crust

1. Pulse the nuts, drained oats, and dates together in a food processor.
2. Add the vanilla, cinnamon, and salt.
3. Blend until a fine "dough."
4. Press into the 9" pie pan and Refrigerate.

Filling

1. Process the sweet potato chunks in the food processor until well blended. For an easier process and smoother filling, push the sweet potatoes through a juicer with the homogenizing blank installed, and then puree with the rest of the ingredients in the food processor.
2. Spread the filling over the crust and refrigerate it for about 3 hours to let it set.

Slice your pie and serve.

CHOCOLATE AVOCADO ICE CREAM

INGREDIENTS:

1 - Banana, peeled and frozen

1 - Large Avocado, peeled and frozen

2 Tbsp - Raw Cacao, or cocoa powder

2 - Dates, pitted and soaked for 20 minutes

Optional: mint leaves, coconut flakes, or peanut butter

DIRECTIONS:

1. Place all ingredients into a food processor and process until broken down and "ice cream consistency" is reached. Add optional add-ins.
2. Use immediately, or let thaw some after airtight freezer storage.

MANGO BLUEBERRY ICE CREAM

INGREDIENTS:

2 - Mangoes, peeled and frozen

2 Cups - Blueberries, frozen

½ Cup - Plant-based milk, unsweetened

2 - Dates, pitted and soaked in water for 20 minutes

Optional: coconut flakes, whole raw blueberries

DIRECTIONS:

1. Place all ingredients into a food processor and process until broken down and "ice cream consistency" is reached. Add optional add-ins.
2. Use immediately, or let thaw some after airtight freezer storage.

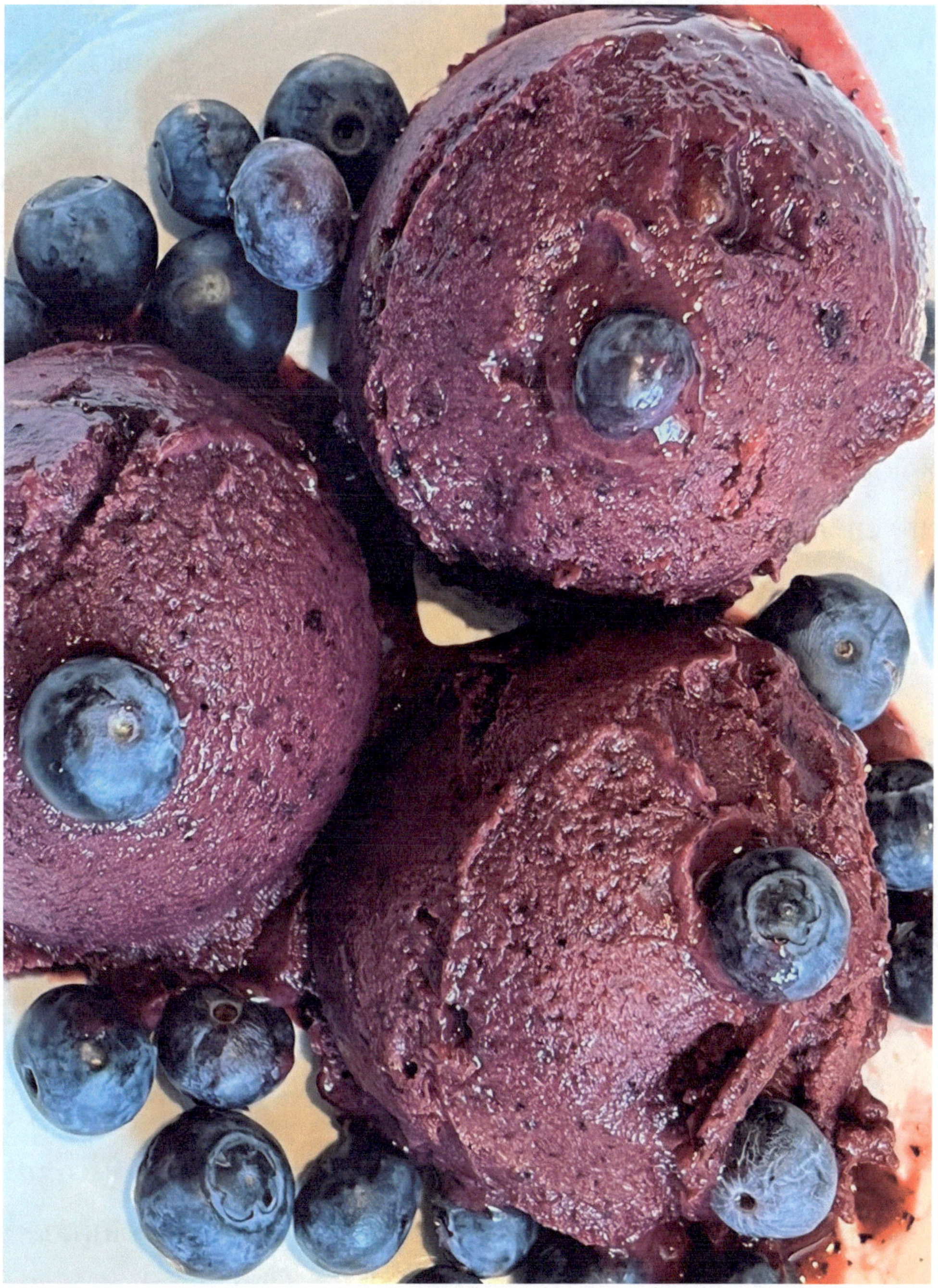

ABOUT THE AUTHOR

Dr. William Richardson M.D., M.S.P.H. is a Public Health and Preventive Medicine specialist who has dedicated his life to getting to the root causes of disease by researching and developing healing strategies to relieve ailments with as natural means as possible.

He has a B.S. in Biochemistry with minors in Physics and Math from the University of Pittsburgh, a Masters in the Science of Public Health - Epidemiology (the study of the distribution and control of disease) from the University of Alabama in Birmingham, and graduated with an M.D. from Temple University, Lewis Katz School of medicine in Philadelphia, Pennsylvania in 1979. He completed three years of training in General and Internal Medicine at Allegheny General Hospital in Pittsburgh, Pennsylvania, and completed a residency in Preventive Medicine at the University of Alabama in Birmingham in 1984.

Dr. Richardson has obtained a great amount of clinical experience working in Emergency Rooms; Urgent Care, Primary Care, Public Health and Occupational Medicine clinics; Psychiatric Hospitals; and his own Preventive Holistic Medical Clinic. He has studied with numerous Complementary-Alternative Physicians, Natural Healers, and Master Herbalists throughout the U.S. and beyond. He has volunteered as a Medical Missionary to Belize - Central America, St. Croix - The Virgin Islands, and Ghana - West Africa. Dr. Richardson has been featured on CNN International News for his economical and innovative treatment of coronary heart disease. He has been a volunteer with the Sickle Cell Foundation of Georgia and had the honor of treating numerous Sickle Cell

Disease (SCD) patients who are often undertreated for the severe, chronic, and acute pain episodes associated with SCD.

He has become a master at successfully using Preventive, Lifestyle, and Integrative Medicine in fighting chronic diseases in a multitude of clients for over three(3) decades such as utilizing Chelation Detoxification Therapy and Nutritional Optimization to allow the body to heal from coronary atherosclerotic heart disease, erectile dysfunction, and autoimmune diseases, including, Sarcoidosis and Severe Eczema. He has utilized amplified pyramid devices that appear to inhibit the growth of lower life forms such as bacteria and mold as part of a comprehensive strategy to allow a patient to heal from gangrene of the foot and avoid amputation.

By doing away with chronic, ongoing ailments with Natural Healing by creating the circumstances for the body to heal itself, many have lived a full life with optimal health. Although some patients may require chronic use of pharmaceuticals, Dr. Richardson's motto is: "I want to make it so you won't need me in the future." He has founded the Advanced Clinics for Preventive Medicine (ACPM) in the Atlanta, Georgia area, where Primary Care and Preventive Medicine Physician and Nurse Practitioner Specialists, Registered Nurses & Dieticians, Herbalists and Holistic Healers work to Prevent, Arrest and Reverse our leading killers.

RESOURCES and INFORMATION

Dr. William Richardson M.D., M.S.P.H. is the founder of the **Advanced Clinics for Preventive Medicine (ACPM)**, an Integrative Medical and Lifestyle Medicine Healing facility serving clients worldwide, based in Atlanta, Georgia for over three decades. Primary care and Preventive Medicine Physicians, Nurse Practitioners, Nurses and Holistic Healers work together to Prevent, Reverse, and Halt the Progression of our leading killers and chronic disease challenges.

ACPM offers the following **Preventive, Integrative and Lifestyle Medicine** approaches to healing a myriad of chronic diseases:
- Comprehensive History, Physical, and Laboratory evaluations.
- Nutritional and Detoxification IV (intravenous) therapies.
- Healing Products and Nutritional Supplements.
- **The Holistic Way Program - Becoming and Staying Well:** Lifestyle Training programs on Healthy Food Preparation, Wellness Coaching & Community, Learning to make your own natural Healing, Personal Care & Cleaning Products, Yoga & Meditation instruction, Herb Walks, and more.

We also offer:
- Fitness Training for all ages
- Lifestyle Nutritional Counseling

  Zoom sessions are available.
- Natural Healing Products, Supplements, and Health Promoting Books

  Sign up for our free newsletter!
- Dr. Richardson is available to speak to groups and for consultations.

Call (770) 419-4471   www.ACPM.net

www.THRIVEhealthandfitness.org

Create the cause for your own Healing and Vitality

REFERENCES

1. Welch R.W. SATIETY: Have we neglected dietary non-nutrients? Proc. Nutr. Soc. 2011; 70(2): 145-54.
2. Barnard N.D., Cohen J., Jenkins D.J., et al. A low-fat vegan diet improves glycemic control and cardiovascular risk factors in a randomized clinical trial in individuals with type 2 diabetes. Diabetes Care. 2006; 29(8): 1777-83.
3. Trapp C.B., Barnard N.D. Usefulness of vegetarian and vegan diets for treating type 2 diabetes. Curr. Diab. Rep. 2010; 10(2): 152-8.
4. Campbell T.C., Parpia B., Chen J. Diet, lifestyle and the etiology of coronary artery disease: The Cornell China Study. Am. J. Cardiol. 1998; 82(10B): 18T-21T.
5. Shaper A.G., Jones K.W. Serum-cholesterol, diet and coronary heart-disease in Africans and Asians in Uganda: 1959I Int. J. Epidemiol. 2012; 41(5): 1221-5.
6. Dennis Burkett M.D. Western Diseases, Their Dietary Prevention and Reversibility. 1994, Humana Press Inc.
7. Donnison C.P. Blood pressure in the African native. Lancet. 1929; 213(5497) : 6-7.
8. Micheal Greger M.D, HOW NOT TO DIE. Flatiron Books, New York, 2015. P.6.
9. Frost G.S., Walton G.E., Swann J.R., et al. Impacts of plant-based foods in ancestral hominin diets on the metabolism and function of gut microbiota in vitro. Molecular Biology. 2014 May 20; 2(3): e00853-14.
10. Sleeth M.L., Thompson E.L., Ford H. E., Zac-Vaghese S.E., Ford H.E., Zac-Vaghese S.E., Frost G. Free fatty acid receptor 2 and nutrient sensing: a proposed role for fiber, fermentable carbohydrates and short-v chain fatty acids in appetite regulation, Nutr. Res. Rev. 2010 Jun; 23(1): 135-45.

11. Kochanek K.D., Murphy S.L., Xu J., Arias E. Mortality in the United States, 2013. NCHS Data Brief 2014; 178.
12. Michael Greger M.D. HOW NOT TO DIE. Flatiron Books, New York 2015. P. 18.
13. Dennis Burkitt M.D. Western Diseases, Their Dietary Prevention and Reversibility. 1984, Humana Press Inc.
14. Threapleton D.E., Greenwood D.C., Evans C.E., et al. Dietary fiber intake and risk of cardiovascular disease: Systemic review and meta-analysis. BMJ. 2013; 347: f6879.
15. Walker A.R., Walker B.F. High high-density lipoprotein cholesterol in African children and adults in a population free of coronary heart disease. Be. Med, J. 1978; 2(6148): 1336-7.
16. Yao B., Fang H., Xu W., et al. Dietary fiber intake and risk of type 2 diabetes: a dose-response analysis of prospective studies. European J. Epidemiol. 2014; 29(2): 79-88.
17. Maskarinec G., Takata Y., Pagano I., et al. Trends and dietary determinants of overweight and obesity in a multi-ethnic population. Obesity (Silver Spring). 2006; 14(4): 717-26.
18. Aune D., Chan D.S., Lan R., et al. Dietary fiber, whole grains and risk of colorectal cancer: Systemic review and dose-response meta-analysis of prospective studies. BMJ. 2011; 343: d6617.
19. Asher M.I., Stewart A.W., Mallol J., et al. Which population level environmental factors are associated with asthma, rhinoconjunctivitis and eczema? Review of the ecological analysis of ISAAC phase one. Respir. Res. 2010; 11:8.
20. Ait-Khaled N., Pearce N., Anderson H.R., et al. Global map of the prevalence of symptoms of rhinoconjunctivitis in children: The International Study of Asthma and Allergies in Childhood ISAAC Phase Three. Allergy. 2009; 64(1); 123-48.
21. Roher A.E., Tyas S.L., Maarouf C.L., et al. Intracranial Atherosclerosis as a contributing factor to Alzheimer's disease-dementia. Alzheimer's Dement. 2011; 7(4): 436-44.

22. Barnard N.D., Bush A.I., Ceccarelli A., et al. Dietary and lifestyle guidelines for the prevention of Alzheimer's disease. Neuronal Aging. 2014; 35 suppl s: S74-8.
23. Jiang W., Ju C., Jiang H., Zhang D. Dairy foods intake and risk of Parkinson's disease: a dose-response meta-analysis of prospective cohort studies. Eur. J. Epidemiol, 2014; 29(9): 613-9.
24. Siddiqui M.K., Sayena M.C., Krishia Murta C.R. Storage of DDT and BMC in adipose tissue of Indian males. Int. J. Environ Anal. Chem. 1981; 10(3-4): 197-204.
25. Lauber S.N., Ali S., Gooberham N.J. The cooked food derived carcinogen 2-amino-1-methyl-6-phenylimidazo [4, 5-6] pyridine is a potent estrogen: a mechanistic basis for its tissue-specific carcinogenicity. Carcinogenesis. 2004; 25(12): 2509-17.
26. Colon I., Caro D., Rosario O., et al. Identification of Phthalates esters in the serum of young Puerto Rican girls with premature breast development. Environ. Health Perspl 200: 108: 895-900.
27. Fredericson B., Muller L., Westerholm R., etal. Human sperm motility is affected by plasticizers and diesel particulate extracts. Pharmacol toxicol. 1993; 128-133.
28. Arnold S.F., et al. Synergistic activation of estrogen receptors with combinations of environmental chemicals. Sci. 1996; 272: 1489-1492.
29. Colborn T., van Saal f.S., Sot A.M. Development effects of endocrine-disrupting chemicals in wildlife and humans. Environ. Health Persps. 1993; 101: 378-84.
30. Frost G.E., Walton G.E., Swann J.R., etal. Impacts of plant-based foods in ancestral hominin diets on the metabolism and function on gut microbiota in vitro. MBio. 2014, May 20; 5(3): e00853-14.
31. Maskarinec G., Takata Y., Pagano I., et al. Trends and dietary determinants of overweight and obesity in a multi-ethnic population. Obesity (Silver Spring). 2006: 14(4): 717-26.
32. Yao B., Fang M., Xu W., et al. Dietary fiber intake and risk of type 2 diabetes: A dose-response analysis of prospective studies. European J. Epidemiol. 2014; 29(2): 79-88.

33. Threapleton D.E., Greenwood D.C., Evans C.E., et al. Dietary fiber intake and risk of cardiovascular disease: systemic review and meta-analysis. BMJ. 2013; 347: f6879.
34. Aune D., Chan D.S., Greenwood D.C., et al. Dietary fiber and breast cancer risk: A systematic review and meta-analysis of prospective studies. Ann Oncol. 2012; 23(6): 1394-402.
35. Aune D., Chan D.S., Lau R., et al. Dietary fiber, whole grains and risk of colorectal cancer: systemic review and dose-response meta-analysis of prospective studies. BMJ. 2011; 343: d6617.
36. Streppel M.T., Arinds L.R., Van 't Veer P., Grobbee D.E., Geleijnse J.M. dietary fiber and blood pressure: a meta-analysis of randomized placebo-controlled trials. Arch. Intern. Med. 2005; 165(2): 150-6.
37. Threapleton D.E., greenwood D.C., Evans C.E., et al. Dietary fiber intake and risk of first troke: a systematic review and meta-analysis. Stroke. 2013; 44(5): 1360-8.
38. Kim Y., Je Y. Dietary fiber intake and total mortality: a meta-analysis of prospective cohort studies. Am J. Epidemiol. 2014; 180(6): 564-73.
39. Mercader J. Mozambican grass seed consumption during the Middle Stone Age. Science. 2009; 326 (5960): 1680-83.
40. Deacon HJ. Planting an idea: An archeology of stone age gatherers in South Africa. S Africa Archaeol Bull. 1993; 48: 86-93.
41. Weiss E, Wetterstrom W, Nadel D, Bar-Yosef O. The broad spectrum revisited: evidence from plant remains. Proc Natl Acad Sci USA. 2004; 101 (26): 9551-55.
42. Santhakumar A.B., Bulmer A.C., Singh I. A review of the mechanisms and effectiveness of dietary polyphenols in reducing oxidative stress and thrombotic risk. J. Hum. Nutr. Diet. 2014; 27(1): 1-21,
43. Chase J.K., Kim J.W., et al. Increased fluid fluid intake and adequate dietary modification may be enough for the successful treatment of uric acid stone. Urolithiasis. 2013; 41(2); 179-82.

44. Nakamura H., Takasawa M., Kashara S., et al. Effects of acute protein loads of different sources on renal function in healthy subjects. Nephron. 1987; 46(1): 37-42.
45. Trinchieri A. Development of a rapid food screener ro assess the potential renal acid load of diet in renal stone formers (LAKE score). Arch. Ital. Uro. Androl. 2012; 84(1); 36-8.
46. Zheng W., Lee S.A. Well-done meal intake, heterocyclic amino exposure and cancer risk. Nutr. Cancer. 2009; 62(4/: 437-46.
47. The Merck Manual, 19th Edition. 2011. Published by Merck, Sharp & Dohme Corp. Robert S. Porter M.D. Editor-in-chief. P. 193.
48. San Joaquin M.A., Appleby P.N., Spencer E.A., Key T.J. Nutrition and lifestyle in relation to bowel movement frequency, a cross-section study of 20,630 men and women in Epic-Oxford. Public Health Nutr. 2004: 7(1): 77-83.
49. Thiebaut A.C.. Jiao L., Silverman D.T., et al. Dietary fatty acids and pancreatic cancer in the NIH-AARP diet and health study. J. Natl. Cancer Inst. 2009; 101(14): 1001-11.
50. Maruyama K., Oshima T., Ohyama K. Exposure to exogenous estrogen through intake of commercial milk produced from pregnant cows. Pediatr. Int. 2010; 52(1): 33-8.
51. Danby F.W. Acne and milk, the diet, myth and beyond. J. Am. Acad. Dermotol. 2005; 52(2): 360-2.
52. Afiche M. Williams P.L., Mediola J., et al. Diary food intake in relation to semen quality and reproductive hormone levels among physically active young men. Human Reproduction 2013; 28(8): 2265-75.
53. Maruyama K., Oshima T., Ohyama K. Exposure to exogenous estrogen through intake of commercial milk produced from pregnant cows. Pediatr. Int. 2010; 25(1): 33-8.
54. Ganmaa D., Li X.M., Qin L.Q., Wang P.Y., Takeda M., Sato A. The experience of Japan as a clue to the etiology of testicular and prostate cancers. Med. Hypothesis. 2003; 60(5): 724-30.

55. Montorsi P., Ravagnani P.M., Galli S., et al. The artery size hypothesis: a macrovascular link between erectile dysfunction and coronary artery disease. Am. J. Cardiol. 2005; 96(12B): 19m-23m.
56. Chiurlo E., D'Amico R., Ratti Granata A.R., et al. Subclinical coronary artery atherosclerosis in patients with erectile dysfunction. J. am. Coll. Cardiol. 2005; 46(8): 1503-6.
57. Fung M.M., Bettencourt R., Barrett-Connor E. Heart disease risk factors predicted erectile dysfunction 25 years later: the Rancho Bernardo Study. J. Am. Coll. Cardiol. 2004; 43(8): 1405-11.
58. Gupta B.P., Murad M.H., Clifton M.M., Prokopl., Et al. The effect of lifestyle modification and cardiovascular risk factor reduction on erectile dysfunction: a systematic review and meta-analysis. Arch Intern Med. 2011; 171(20): 1797-803.
59. Campbell T.C., Parpia B., Chen J. Diet, lifestyle and the etiology of coronary artery disease: the Cornell China study. Am. J. Cardiol. 1998; 82(10B): 18T-21T.
60. Aldenir M., Okulu E. Neseliglu S., Erel O., Kayigil O. Pistachio diet improves erectile function parameters and serum lipid profiles in patients with erectile dysfunction. Int. J. Impot. Res. 2011; 23(1): 32-8.
61. Esposito K., Ciotola M., Maiorino M. I., et al. Hyperlipidemia and sexual function in premenopausal women J. Sex. Med. 2009; 6(6): 1696-703.
62. Trewell M.C., Burkitt D.P. Western Diseases: Their Emergence and Prevention. Boston: Howard University Press; 1981.
63. Dr. John McDougall, M.D. The Starch Solution. Rodale, Inc. New York, NY; 2012, p 42.
64. Lindberg S., et al. Low serum insulin in traditional Pacific Islanders - the Kitava Study. Metabolism. 1999 Oct; 48(10): 1216-19.ification and cardiovascular risk factor reduction on erectile dysfunction: a systematic review and metaanalysis. Arch. Intern. Med. 2011; 171(20): 1797-803.

65. Roberts W.C. The cause of atherosclerosis. Nutr. Clin. Pract. 2008; 23(5): 464-7.

The Author and Grandson, Adeyemi W. Franklin.
Photo by Mr. Glen Gilkey

Make Time for Your Wellness.

Never Give Up!

Be Positive All the Time.

A family tie is like a tree, it can bend but it cannot break. ~ African proverb

Dr. William Emikola Richardson
Quinnie Adejiwa Cook-Richardson
Folasuyi Richardson-Franklin
Akinbola Richardson
Olatunde Richardson
Orisamola Richardson
Adeshola Richardson
Olage Richardson

Made in the USA
Columbia, SC
28 May 2024